D0901894

What About Nancy?

what about Nancy?

and other
TRUE
LIFE
STORIES
to reignite
your hope

RAY & NANCY PAINTER

*includes daily devotionals
to strengthen your faith*
by Denise Monson

illustrations by mika monson

What about Nancy? and other TRUE LIFE STORIES to reignite your hope

Copyright © 2023 Ray & Nancy Painter / Denise Monson
All rights reserved. No part of this book may be reproduced in any form without written permission of the copyright owners. To request permissions, contact whataboutnancy@gmail.com

These are our memories, from our perspective, and we have tried to represent events as faithfully as possible.

Unless otherwise noted, Scripture is taken from the New King James Version®. Copyright © 1982 by Thomas Nelson. Used by permission. All rights reserved.

Other Scripture references are from the following sources: Scripture quotations marked (TLB) are taken from *The Living Bible,* copyright © 1971 by Tyndale House Foundation. Used by permission of Tyndale House Publishers, Carol Stream, Illinois 60188. All rights reserved. Scripture quotations marked (ESV) are from The ESV® Bible (The Holy Bible, English Standard Version®), copyright © 2001 by Crossway, a publishing ministry of Good News Publishers. Used by permission. All rights reserved.

Published by Bright Door Publishing, Delavan, WI
Printed in the United States
Cover design by Denise Monson
Illustrations by Mika Monson

ISBN 979-8-9873605-1-4 (hardback)
ISBN 979-8-9873605-0-7 (paperback)
Library of Congress Control Number: 2023907365

Contents

Introduction

Part I - What About Nancy?

By Ray and Nancy Painter

If you've lost your hope; if you're hurting and feeling alone, or if you just love a good romantic story—read on!

Have you ever felt like your life went haywire, like someone pulled the rug out from under your feet? Questions bombard your mind—*How did this happen? Is it my fault? What do I do now?*

Maybe you've experienced a devastating divorce or an unexpected, too-soon death in your family. In those times of darkness, you may wonder if life is worth living or if you can ever be happy again.

Nancy's story is real. Deserted and overwhelmed with the responsibility of two teenagers to raise on her own, how would they survive? How could she and her children ever recover from this loss?

Ray was devastated by the loss of his wife. It happened so quickly. She was young and full of life. It was unfair. He was filled with sorrow and confusion, and at times, anger.

1

In this book, they share their stories hoping it will encourage others that there can be life after loss. You can go on!

Part II – True Stories with Devotionals

Stories by Nancy Painter, unless otherwise indicated

This part of the book includes 30 true stories of God showing up in various ways to reveal His love and guidance. Each story has a devotional and prayer to encourage and uplift the reader. These could be used for personal or group Bible studies. For a free 6-week group study guide, visit www.whataboutnancy.com.

Part III – Legacy Stories

By Nancy Painter, unless otherwise indicated

This section contains five true family legacy stories. You are here for a purpose and your life matters! What will your legacy be?

Part IV – Jesus is Asking

Are you discouraged with religion and looking for a relationship? You can turn to this section before you even begin!

Chapter One
Nancy's Prayer

[Nancy]

Bye mom! Love you!" my teenagers, Mary and Richie, were off to school and suddenly the house was quiet.

I cherished the peaceful forty-five minutes I had alone before leaving for work, but it went by too quickly. Patting our dog Shadow on the head, I headed down the stairs to the garage of our bi-level home and climbed into my Chevy Blazer. It was an old gas guzzler, but it was paid for and felt comfortable to me.

Music from my favorite radio station, WFEN, flooded my car and I sang along as I headed down the road. It seemed to be a normal, ordinary day. I had come to love "normal."

It was a peaceful drive with rural homes, open green fields, and very little traffic along the way. In the spring, I'd often see horses with their young colts frolicking through the fields. It made my heart happy. I loved working as the receptionist at our church and living so close to my daughter, son-in-law, and my grandchildren. A police officer and his wife lived next door. I felt safe. I was free from the chaos that had led me to move to the small country town of Winnebago four years earlier.

Winnebago had one grocery store, two gas stations, a library, a post office, two great pizza places, a family restaurant, and of course, a McDonalds. They were all within about eight blocks of each other. When we first moved there, I stopped at the grocery store, and one of the young men who was bagging my groceries took my cart, walked me to the car, and unloaded them all in the trunk for me. He did not want a tip!

Who does that? This town is incredible! It was true what the sign said at the corner as you entered off the highway: "Wonderful Winnebago!"

As I continued my drive to work, the cell phone rang interrupting my thoughts.

"Hi, Mom!" It was Denise. She was not only my precious daughter but had become a trusted friend. We often talked and sometimes prayed together on our way to work in the mornings. She was my firstborn, followed by my son, Joe, who also was grown and on his own. Then came Mary and Richie, my teenagers, who had lived through the nightmare with me. The move to Winnebago was for them. I had been homeschooling when everything fell apart, and I wanted to put them in a small school so that it wouldn't be as hard of an adjustment for them.

"Hi, sweetheart."

We talked for a while and then she said, "Mom, I was praying for you this morning, and I prayed for a Boaz to come into your life." I knew of the remarkable love story of Ruth and Boaz in the Bible. Boaz was a protector and provider to Ruth, who had been through a tragic and devastating loss.

"What! Why would you pray something like that, Denise?" My harsh tone with my daughter surprised me. "Why didn't you ask me about this? You know I'm happy now."

"Mom, I hadn't planned on praying this, but I felt God impressed it on my heart,"

"Okay, honey." My voice softened. "But you know I don't need a man in my life. I'm happy."

Denise and I talked a little longer and then she said, "I love you, Mom. Have a good day."

"Love you too, sweetheart. Talk to you later." There was no more singing as I drove to work. Silence seemed to engulf me, and a heaviness replaced my joy.

God, why would you put that on her heart? I don't understand. You rescued me! You took care of me and made a way for me to escape all the turmoil and pain. You've helped my heart to heal. I can't go through this again! I'm happy. I don't want another man. It just brings heartbreak! I can't do it!

As soon as I ended my prayer, thoughts of past events bombarded my mind. I didn't want to go back in time, but memories came flooding in as I remembered my first marriage. It dissolved after my husband told me he had fallen in love with someone else. We had been married for twenty-four years and I loved him deeply. This loss caused me to fall into a severe depression. It felt like the world was swirling around me and I was in a capsule—functioning, but not really there. My sleep was sporadic, and my appetite was gone. One morning after stepping on the scale, I was surprised to see that my weight had dropped to 105 pounds, not a healthy weight for my 5'4" frame. I wondered how I would go on.

While struggling with this loss, I worked at a law office and would sometimes walk over to a small nearby grocery store during my lunch hour. On one particularly beautiful day, I wanted to get out of the office and away from people, so I decided to head there and get some fresh air.

I went into the store and walked toward the back. At the time, they had a bakery, and as I looked down into the glass-covered case displaying all their pastries, I spotted cherry cobblers. Cherry pie is one of my favorites, and I felt hungry for the first time in a while. I looked in my purse and found I had just enough change for one piece. I said a silent prayer. *Lord, I'm hungry today. Would you please give me a big piece of cobbler?* I then told the clerk what I wanted and paid her.

She handed me the little, white bakery bag, and I walked outside and opened it. To my surprise, there were two pieces of cobbler in the bag! My heart jumped, but I knew I needed to inform the clerk of the mistake, as I had only paid for one. So, I walked back in and told her what had happened. She smiled at me. "That's okay. Keep them."

I walked outside and began to thank God. I was praising Him for answering my prayer! In the middle of my praise, He interrupted me with the words, *I care for you*. It wasn't an audible voice, but it was real and unmistakably God. I will never forget that moment. Joy and love and peace flooded my heart. The God who runs the universe saw my pain and reached down and whispered to me!

6

Everything didn't miraculously become wonderful again, but something changed inside of me. I felt the courage and strength to go on. From that moment on, I knew deep in my heart that God was with me and cared about all that concerned me!

For the first time in my life, I learned from Him about real forgiveness, and I distinctly remember the day I chose to forgive my ex-husband. The Bible verse* that says we must forgive in order to be forgiven bothered me because I didn't think I could forgive, and I didn't want to!

I lay on my bed wrestling with it all and finally, I said, "God, this isn't fair! I didn't do anything wrong! I loved him!" Of course, I had done things wrong, but it was how I felt at the time.

The moment I said those words, I heard Jesus say in my spirit, *Did I do anything wrong?* His presence filled the room as I pictured him on the cross bleeding and dying for me. I felt no condemnation, only love. I said, "I'm sorry, Lord! I choose to forgive." I didn't feel like I'd forgiven him. It was a decision, not a feeling, but I began to heal. There were many times I would remind myself that I had chosen forgiveness, but over time it became easier and the pain lessened.

After being married for such a long time, I did miss sharing life with someone. Even though I felt my heart had healed, I was not interested in dating, but being a single mom was very difficult. I had full responsibility for our bi-level home in Rockford. I had opened and was operating a daycare in the lower level of the home so I could work at home and be with my children.

*Matthew 6:14-15

One day, about two years after the divorce, my basement flooded during a terrible rainstorm. It happened fast while I still had children in my daycare. I was frantically trying to keep all the children safe while calling their parents. It looked like our road might become impassable. Thankfully, it didn't, but my home was an awful mess, and it was all overwhelming to me.

Some friends from my church came to help and brought along a couple of men I didn't know. They all worked very hard to help restore my daycare, but I still had to work from my living room. One of the men asked my daughter Denise if he could surprise me while I was on vacation with my family for a few days. He worked hard to get the daycare functioning so I could move it back to the lower level. I was so happy when I saw all that he had done to make everything better for me and my daycare children.

His kindness caught my attention. We became friends and the friendship grew into love. When he talked to me about marriage, I was hesitant, but eventually, after praying, I said yes. We were married at our church a few months later. He was a good man. He was not afraid to work, and he also was more than willing to help others. For a time, we did daycare together and even though it was hard work, we managed to make it fun sometimes. It was during this time that an opportunity came for us to adopt one of the children who had come through my daycare. Richie was almost eleven years old when he joined our family. We installed an above-ground pool in the backyard and the kids loved it. Life was good.

One day a friend told us about a job opening in a distribution company. We decided it was a good opportunity. My husband applied and was hired. He worked hard, and it didn't take long until he became a supervisor. But due to a downturn in the economy, he lost his job. He became discouraged. It was hard to find another job, but he eventually took a job as a truck driver. Trucking wasn't a good lifestyle with him being on the road and away from home. Eventually, he started listening to music from his past and drinking, which led to his former life of drugs. I was aware of his past, but he was a changed man when I met him and had come so far. It seemed that he had overcome it all. It was frightening to watch him slide back into that world.

I felt like a terrible wife because sometimes I would hide my billfold at night before going to bed. I was afraid if I didn't hide my money, it would all be missing in the morning. There were nights that I would wake up and find my husband gone. When I called his phone, I'd get no answer. I felt abandoned. I was scared, not only for me but for him. I didn't know where he was or what he was doing, but I knew it wasn't good. Not knowing when and if he would return was torment.

Possessions went missing from our home. I went to the pawn shop with him to buy back our things because I loved him and wanted to believe we were going to make it through this. The pawn shop was a dark and dirty place with bars over the window to protect the owner. I wanted only to get our things back and get out of there. But eventually, I'd find things missing again, even his wedding ring was gone. The nightmare continued as he got lost in the world of drugs. It changed him from the kind and responsible man I knew into someone I could no longer trust.

One day I walked out to the mailbox and found about eight notices from the bank. Checks had been written to various places, mostly gas stations and grocery stores, on our account. There wasn't enough money in the account, so they all bounced. It surprised me that I felt peace instead of panic. I knew what I had to do. I was no longer confused. I had to file papers for divorce. I had to separate myself and my children from this chaos. Even though I knew it was time, I talked with my pastor and close friends before filing the papers, but after eight years, it was over. I was done with any thoughts of marriage ever again!

But as I continued my drive to work, other memories began to surface in my mind of all the miracles God did during those times. I had watched as He did miracle after miracle for my children and me.

Shortly before my second husband and I separated, I noticed that the number eleven was getting my attention. I would look at the clock and it would be 11:11 or 1:11. I would look at the car in front of me while driving and it would have 111 on its license plate. It would show up in many different ways.

At first, I didn't think it was anything more than a coincidence. Then one night my daughter Mary walked into my bedroom and said, "Look, Mom, it's 11:11. Without knowing, she had brought my attention to this number again. Finally, one morning my friend Ann and I decided to pray and ask God if He was trying to say something to me. The next day my friend Margie called me. Her husband had gotten an email from someone who had experienced the

10

same thing. This person did some studying to try to figure it out and discovered the number 11 meant transition and revelation.

I didn't have any idea what that could mean or knowledge of the changes that were about to happen. I had been working part-time and homeschooling Mary and Richie. When my ex-husband and I separated, I knew I would have to find a full-time job to support us.

And then the miracles began...

Margie called one day and told me that she thought there might be a job opening at our church. When I called Pastor Brad, who oversaw hiring employees, he asked me to come in to apply. My heart jumped!

After arriving at church for the interview, I sat in the car for a moment. I felt inadequate and nervous. *God help me! I really need a job in order to move and get another home. If this is where you want me, please open the door for me. I trust you!* With that, I headed in for the interview.

After talking to Pastor Brad for a while, he looked at me and said, "When can you start and what salary do you think you'd like to start at?" I don't know if my face showed it, but I was flabbergasted!

Did he just hire me? Yes, I think he did! I drove home amazed and so thankful! I now had a full-time job with benefits!

I started to look for a small town to move to as I knew the transition from homeschooling would be hard for Mary and Richie. The town of Winnebago appealed to me. Margie lived there and loved it.

In order to move, we had to get the house ready to sell but there were several unfinished projects to complete. I had lived in that house for over twenty years.

In my Bible reading one morning, God gave me a scripture, "Be strong and courageous and get to work. Don't be frightened by the size of the task, for the Lord my God, is with you: He will not forsake you. He will see to it that everything is finished correctly.... Others with skills of every kind will volunteer..." (1 Chronicles 28:20-21 TLB). It spoke straight to my heart. I was thankful God was encouraging me.

A day or two after I read this verse, my phone rang. It was Margie. She and her family wanted to come over and help get our home ready to sell. There was so much work to be done. One of her sons, Cody, who didn't even know us, wanted to help.

One day while working on the house, we realized we needed an electrician, so we all gathered around the kitchen table, joined hands, and prayed. I walked out the back door, and there was a man working on our neighbor's home. I said to him, "Are you an electrician?"

"I am. Do you need an electrician?"

"I do!"

He followed me into the house so I could show him what I needed to be done. We all stood amazed as he offered to do the work for a much lower price than normal, asking me not to share with my neighbor what he was charging me.

After all the work was completed, Denise made up a flyer and we advertised an open house. Nothing happened at first, so we advertised it a second time. While praying, I felt the Lord put it on my heart to not just let people look around, but to share with them the positive things I loved about the house, the drawbacks, and any projects that needed to be completed. I did that and we had an offer on the same night of the open house!

One day while driving around Winnebago on my lunch hour, I found a home that was for sale by the owner. It looked beautiful to me. I called the number on the sign and set an appointment to see the house. I took the kids with me, and we all immediately loved it.

Richie said, "Mom, you gotta buy this house!" I wanted to, but it was over my budget. When I told the owners, I couldn't afford the price, they offered to reduce it by $10,000. They also allowed us to move in before we had closed the deal and signed the papers.

The people who were buying my house in Rockford offered to help us move, along with my family and friends. On the day of our move, Margie and her family brought over a cattle trailer to haul all our furniture to our new home. That made me laugh, but it worked just fine.

As we were doing the final packing and leaving the house, I went to my car to be alone and broke down crying. Some of the tears were from the sadness of leaving our long-time home with so many precious memories and some were tears of gratitude for the faithfulness of God in helping us through all of this and making a way for us through this mess.

One day as the three of us were talking about all of this, Richie quoted a line from a movie he had seen. Richie said, "This is my family. It's little and broken, but still good, yeah, still good."

It touched my heart. We were broken but we still had love in our family. It had been an agonizing, yet wonderous time as we saw God "part the Red Sea" for us. My heart had healed and we were happy again.

* * *

So, that morning as I pulled into the parking lot at work, and considered Denise's Boaz prayer, I cried out, "God help me! I love you! You have always been there for me. I'm scared. I want your will, but I think there's something wrong with me. Having two failed marriages is so wrong. Look at my sisters! They both have stayed married forever—'til death do us part—but I can't seem to know how to make a marriage work. God, I've tried! I'm just not enough. I'm not enough!"

As I sat in the car, I agonized over this surrender. How could I say no to allowing God into this part of my life? But how could I say yes to opening my heart to a Boaz?

Finally, I prayed, "God, if you want me to have a Boaz in my life, I'm willing. It's not what I want, but I trust you more than anything." The seriousness of what I had prayed hit me. Would God expect me to go through another marriage? Maybe He was testing me to see if I was willing.

That's it! He just wants to know if I would be willing. With that, I headed into work.

Chapter Two
Ray's Prayer

[Ray]

I walked outside our home and screamed up to the heavens, "No, God, no!" My heart was shattered. We had fought hard and believed God for Jan to get well, but in the end, she was gone. She died that day in our home. We had been married for thirteen years.

As much as I tried, I didn't understand what all had happened and what I was to do next. Cancer is not bigger than my God, so why did this happen? I never thought she would be gone before me. She was eight years younger than me, only fifty-seven years old. Why was I left here alone? What was I supposed to do now?

We had fought cancer once before. The year we were married, right before the wedding, I was diagnosed with cancer.

I was at work when I got the call from the doctor. After giving me the results from the tests, he said if I didn't have surgery I would probably die. When I declined surgery right away, he yelled at me through the phone, "My God, man. You've got cancer!"

This resonated and shook me to the core. Fear gripped my heart like I'd never experienced before. I went back to work building a boiler room in a brand-new school. My responsibility was to put all the controls and pipes into the boiler room. How was I going to do this? My mind was reeling. I tried to be careful not to make any mistakes because I was not thinking right. I was gripped with fear.

For the next three days, I fought that fear day and night. I could hardly sleep. Finally, at church, I talked to my pastor. I told him what was going on, and he suggested that I read a book by Charles Capps called *How to Have Faith in Your Faith.* I bought it from the bookstore in our church and started to read it every chance I could get. I had to get rid of this fear!

One wintery lunchtime, I was sitting in my cold car wondering what I was going to do because I had reached the end of the book, but I was still fighting fearful thoughts. But when I looked down, I noticed a footnote at the end of the book which said that if all else fails to pray in the spirit continually.

I could do that! So, I started praying in the Holy Spirit fervently. Every moment I was not reading blueprints and doing things that required a lot of thinking, I was praying in the Spirit—when I was welding, while I was jogging, or whatever I was doing. For three days, I prayed constantly. I never quit until I went to sleep at night.

Suddenly, I noticed something welling up inside. I felt stronger and stronger as I kept praying, and soon I found myself thinking, *Come on, devil! You can't take me out with that cancer! You're not going to win!*

I talked to Jan, my fiancée at the time, and she said, "Well, let's get a second opinion now."

I felt my faith was working now, so we got a second opinion from another specialist who was highly recommended. He examined me and said, "I can't seem to find anything wrong. I'll take a look at the biopsy that they pulled, and we'll examine that."

He called me a couple of days later and said, "Yes, you've got cancer, and it's the fast-growing kind. We need to operate immediately."

I said, "Doc, I'm getting married in fifteen days. I can't do that! I'm going on a three-week honeymoon. Besides that, Jesus heals."

He said, "We need to operate now. If we don't operate soon, you won't make it. It will be all through your body." With that, he hung up the phone.

I told Jan about it, and we decided to believe God for a healing, complete healing, and not worry about it.

One day as I was getting ready for work and listening to the radio, I heard a song by Steven Curtis Chapman, "I Will Be Here." It was a wedding song, and I felt the Lord say to me, *I want you to sing this song at your wedding*.

I sat there and cried. "Lord, you know this will be in faith because I've got this cancer that's going to kill me if I'm not healed." But finally, I said, "Okay, Lord. I will sing this song."

So, I bought a CD that had the song on one side and just the music on the other. In the middle of our wedding ceremony, I sang that song to Jan—I will be here. It was a testimony that, through thick and thin, whatever might come our way, I would be there for her.

We got married and went on our honeymoon on July fifteenth. We were riding my motorcycle and pulling a small pop-up tent camper behind it with all our things in it. I had to build an extra car-top carrier for it because—bless their hearts—most women need a lot of stuff!

The first place we went to was Niagara Falls and were there for two days when we decided to go swimming in this great big one-acre pool. No one was there. No one was swimming that day. It was empty and had a big pier jutting into it. We swam for a while, but I had made arrangements for us to go to the Needlepoint Restaurant on the Canadian side of Niagara Falls that night. People had told us to set the appointment for eight o'clock so we could see the lighting of the Falls. It was beautiful to see it from way up high like that.

At about six o'clock, Jan went to take a shower to get ready for our supper. I decided to wait at the pool for her. I was leaning up against a brick shower building and talking to the Lord and all of a sudden, the Lord spoke up on the inside of me and said, *Go read Isaiah 53:4 and 5*. For a faith person, I should have known what that said, but I didn't. I wasn't aware of the Word of God that well.

I headed down to our campsite and sat underneath the porch of the tent. I opened up my Bible and started reading it. "Surely He has borne our griefs and carried our sorrows; Yet we esteemed Him stricken, smitten by God, and afflicted. But He was wounded for our transgressions, He was bruised for our iniquities; the chastisement for our peace was upon Him, and by His stripes we are healed."

After reading the verse, I noticed that my study Bible referenced the words "griefs" and "sorrows." I decided to look it up to see what they were referring to and found it was translated as "sickness and pain." I started getting tears in my eyes. I said, "Jesus, I know you did this for me. I can receive it right now." I reached up and grabbed the cord hanging on the tent and said, "I am going to take it right now." (It was a symbol of reaching out and taking His promise to me.) Nothing, no bells, no whistles, nothing happened that I could see or feel, but that night I could tell—things were different.

From that moment on, I had a joyous, wonderful vacation. It was a wonderful honeymoon for three weeks, and when I got back to the doctor, he said, "What did you do? Did you get radiation or treatments or something?" I said, "No, I told you, doc, Jesus heals."

"Well, Jesus—healer—or whatever. We'll keep an eye on it and we'll keep testing and make sure that it's gone and that it won't come back." It didn't come back. We won that battle together. But this battle was different. I had lost her. My heart was broken.

***

The days that followed Jan's death seemed unreal to me. My family and friends were there for me, but the house was empty now. The quietness was overwhelming. I didn't understand why I was now alone, but I knew one thing—I needed to get away from the empty house. I had sold our trucking business when Jan got sick; she had done all the bookkeeping, and she became too ill to continue. There was nothing keeping me there anymore. Since I was a retired pipefitter, I decided to take the welding test at a nearby power plant, and I passed. I left as soon as there was a job

19

opening. It was a relief to go back to work again, to be with people, earning a good paycheck, and working through my loss.

Come December, I was working at the Perry Nuclear Power Plant in Cleveland, Ohio when our supervisor told us the job was shutting down for two weeks so we could go home for Christmas and New Year's to spend time with our families.

"Go home," he said. But the thought of returning home did not bring the excitement I would normally feel. Everything was different now.

I gathered my things, left work, and headed down the road trying to keep my mind occupied with anything but my arrival at my home in Byron, Illinois.

After several hours of driving, I turned onto the long, gravel driveway and drove over the hill that hid my home from the road. I saw my farm in the distance. It was a cozy home with a stone fireplace. Originally, it had been a pony express stop, but eventually, the rooms were expanded, and a porch was added to the house. I loved this place, with all the land and my oversized garage, where I had repaired so many trucks and equipment.

I drove over the creek that flowed through my property. The small pond glistened in the distance as I pulled my truck up to the end of the gravel road. I threw the truck into park and grabbed my duffle bag. As I got out, I stopped and stood there, taking it all in—the openness of the adjacent farmer's field with no neighbors in sight, the quietness and serenity of this land.

But my heart felt as barren and stripped as the winter fields now were. It was always beautiful here no matter the season, but an overwhelming sorrow hit me. There was no one waiting at the door to greet me.

I walked the stone pathway to the small porch that opened into the kitchen. After being on the road for a few months, it was good to be back home, but as I dropped my things on the kitchen table and walked into the front room, the emptiness followed me and filled every space I entered.

I spent as much time with family as possible trying to fill my time with activities and surrounding myself with people I loved. Coming back home after Christmas get-togethers without Jan was heartbreaking.

One day as I stood in the living room alone in the silence, I felt nervous because, while I was away, the Lord had laid it on my heart to go to Bible college. It all seemed so overwhelming to me. God had called me to go to Bible school years ago, but it just never seemed like the right time. Even though I was in my sixties I knew the time was now, but I didn't want to go alone. My heart was heavy, and my mind was muddled.

I decided to go into my bedroom and pray. I knelt down by the bed. Even though I didn't understand everything, He was still my God, and I knew that I needed Him. As I prayed and talked to the Lord about various things going on in my life, I had to ask Him about going to Bible school. I told Him I did not want to go alone. I would like to have a wife to go with me.

As clear as a bell, I heard God say, "What about Nancy?" It was so clear that it seemed God had spoken audibly to me. I told the Lord, "Wow! That's a good idea! I hadn't even thought about her. I'll go talk to her."

Immediately, I jumped up from my knees and headed straight to our church where Nancy worked as the receptionist. She was someone I had known casually for many years. From the first time I met her, she had made an impression on me. There was something about her that was special to me. Whenever I'd see her, I was drawn to her, but it never seemed that we were meant to be. But now the Lord had spoken clearly! I was excited as I pulled into the church parking lot. I had no doubts; I knew Nancy was going to be my wife!

Chapter Three
The Encounter

[Nancy]

I put the Boaz prayer that Denise had prayed in the back of my mind and went on with my life. With the full responsibility of two teenagers and trying to keep everything in our home running smoothly, it wasn't hard for me to forget about it. Then one day while I was working, a man appeared at the counter of the church office. He attended our church, and I knew who he was, but as he stood in front of me, I felt embarrassed because I couldn't remember his name.

Being the receptionist, it was important to remember people's names, but every once in a while, a person's name would just escape me! Thankfully, my co-worker, Margaret, sat at the desk behind me. There was a half partition between us, but if she saw I was in trouble, she was always there to help. I had grown to love her dearly. She was a wonderful woman of faith. Even though I was older than her, I sometimes felt like she looked out for me, as if I was her younger sister. When I started working at Faith Center,

I was in the middle of my divorce. I was very broken, but everyone was so supportive.

Margaret had a big heart and she taught me much. Once I was telling her how I never wanted to have a dysfunctional family. I wanted my husband to recover from his addiction. My hope was to be married forever and to live an "Ozzie and Harriet" kind of life. They had their problems, but it always worked out in the end. As I finished talking, Margaret looked me straight in the eyes. She had an authoritative tone in her voice, "Nancy, you are not a dysfunctional family! You and Mary and Richie love each other very much and you are getting along just fine! That makes you a functional family! Did you know that, from what I've read, Ozzie and Harriet's family was pretty dysfunctional? Nancy, that was just a television show." I hugged her and thanked her, but something inside of me changed that day. Her words were life to me!

Now, as I looked over the divider, Margaret knew I needed help and quietly told me his name. I smiled a "thank you" to her. The name of the man standing in front of me at the counter was Ray. He was asking to see one of the pastors so I called his office.

"Pastor, Ray Painter would like to see you."

"Sure, send him on down to my office."

Ray walked down the hall, and I went on with my work. Just a few minutes later, he was back at the counter, talking to me. I don't remember what the conversation was about.

He sure is hanging out here awhile, I thought, but shrugged it off. People often tended to stay and visit awhile. I knew he had lost his wife several months before, and I thought he probably doesn't know what to do with himself and just needs to be with people. So, we visited a little longer.

I noticed he was writing something down. He then came around from the counter, opened the office door, and came up to my desk. He looked tall as he stood in front of me. Smiling, he handed me the paper.

"I thought maybe you might like to talk sometime. This is my number."

"Oh, okay, thanks."

Then he left. I sat there dumbfounded. Alarms went off inside of me! *What is this about?* I knew I would never call him. It wasn't that he wasn't a nice guy, I just didn't do that. I was not interested in starting a relationship with anyone! I hadn't dated since my divorce, over four years earlier, and I didn't want to. There were a couple of guys who showed interest, nice guys, but I had some serious walls around me. I was always polite, but I had no intention of getting involved with anyone.

Something seemed different about this encounter. My feelings and my thoughts were mixed up. I didn't understand what was happening, but for some reason, a part of me quietly hoped I might see him again.

As I drove home that night, I tried not to think about the visit with Ray. After all, there was a lot to get done after work, and it was very frightening for me to even entertain the idea of a man in my life. There was a part of me that wanted to believe in an everlasting love, but it hadn't proven true in my life.

I need to 'play it safe' and stay single for the rest of my life. I need to quit thinking about all this. I turned my thoughts to getting supper ready for Mary and Richie. I wanted to hear about their day and not think anymore about the past or even the future.

The next morning, I decided I needed to talk with Pastor Lyon about Ray. Our conversation bothered me for some reason, and I felt he would be back. When Pastor came into the office, I asked him if when he had a few minutes, I could talk with him.

"Sure, Nancy, come in right now and we can talk." He had a fatherly kindness. I loved this man of God and his wife dearly. They had been there for me and my family so many times over the years. I even discovered that when I was a little girl, he had pastored the church where I first asked Jesus into my heart. Many years later I found myself drawn to attend Faith Center, not knowing he was now pastoring this church.

I felt so honored to work at and be a part of this church and to see how gracious and kind our pastors were on an everyday level. Pastor Lyon was a pastor to pastors all over the world. Sometimes a pastor from another church would just drop in and ask to spend a few minutes talking with him. I never knew what the conversations were about, but I knew they valued his advice and wisdom, just as I did.

So, this day, I looked at Pastor Lyon and said, "Ray Painter came in yesterday and we talked for a while. He gave me his phone number and asked me to call him sometime. I don't plan on calling him, but I wanted to ask you—Is there any reason I should run?"

He looked at me, thought a little, and then said, "I can't think of any reason, Nancy." We talked for a while and I thanked him for his help and went back to my work.

As strange as it seems, there was a "knowing" inside of me that my life was changing. I wanted to talk to my pastor as I felt shaken by it all. I wasn't sure what was going to happen next, but I had a feeling that Ray Painter would be back, and I needed to somehow be prepared. I wasn't sure how I was supposed to do that, but talking to my pastor brought me some assurance and peace.

***

Our church's New Year's Eve service was only a couple of days after Ray had shown up at the office and handed me his phone number. It was a wonderful time to be in church, letting go of the old year and bringing in the new. As I stood there singing and worshipping, a thought abruptly entered my mind—*I wonder if Ray is here.* I didn't really want to think about that, and it bothered me that it had entered my mind. I dismissed it and decided to get my focus back on worship.

I had volunteered to work the last two hours of the service in the office. I got myself a small plate of snacks and headed back to the office to relieve Kellie, who had covered the first part of the service. Kellie was the Office Manager and had become a dear and supportive friend. She encouraged me to grow and trusted me with new responsibilities. She helped me to believe in myself again because I knew she believed in me.

I sat down and got settled at my desk, but when I looked up, there stood Ray. I remember he had a big smile on his face. My first thought was, *I need to get away*, but that was impossible because I was working. There was a

27

part of me that wanted to run, but then the other part of me was glad he was there. I had instantly lost my appetite to nerves as I looked at the snack before me, wondering what was wrong with me!

The next thing I knew, he opened the office door and came in, and stood by my desk. As I looked up at him, he seemed very tall and his presence seemed to fill the room. The sign on the door said, "Authorized Personnel", but he either didn't notice or it didn't matter to him.

As we talked, he told me that he would be leaving for work out of town soon and that he was a retired pipe fitter, but after his wife passed away, he had decided he needed to get away from his home and the memories. He was working in Ohio and had taken a break to come home for Christmas.

He talked and smiled a lot. I found myself laughing as we talked. He definitely had a sense of humor.

I gave up any thought of snacking as we visited. He enjoyed kidding, or, as he called it, "bumping people" to see their response. Then he'd smile, and his smile was so contagious, accompanied by a dimple on the right side of his face. We watched some of the service but talked quite a bit. He would say something, and I was surprised by his forthrightness, not always knowing how to respond.

It was time to go home, and he waited for me as I closed up the office. He walked me to my car, opened the door for me, and smiled as we said, "goodnight." As I headed home, I realized that he had asked for my number, and I had given it to him! This was unsettling and at the same time a little exciting, Then I remembered he was leaving town, and I relaxed as I finished my drive home.

Chapter Four
The Phone Call

[Ray]

My time at home was ended and it was time to head back to work. I packed my bags, closed up the house, and hooked up the fifth-wheel camper for the drive to Ohio. I needed to get there in time to start a new assignment working at a nuclear power plant. The drive gave me plenty of opportunities to ponder the last few days and my time with Nancy.

Thinking back, I was so thankful that after my first visit with Nancy, I had called and talked with David Meyer. David is Jan's son and my stepson. He and his wife Lindy were pastoring a church in Illinois. During our conversation, I told him about my encounter with the Lord and what the Lord had told me about Nancy.

I shared with him that I had gone to the church right away so I could talk with her and that it had gone okay, but I didn't come away with her phone number. I was a little discouraged because after talking with her, I hadn't felt she was ready to give me her phone number. She was polite, but I could tell she was guarded. I decided it would be better not to ask for her number. I didn't think it would be received well, so I gave her my number, hoping she might call me.

David said, "She ain't going to call you, Ray; she's old school. She'll never call you back."

I knew David was right and determined that somehow, I was going to connect with her before I left to go back on the road. So come New Year's Eve, I headed to church. I wanted to be in the service, but I also wanted to see Nancy before I left town.

During the break, I was rubbernecking all over the church looking for her. There were probably about a thousand people there, but I was determined to find her.

Another break and I still couldn't find her.

Then it dawned on me! *I bet she's in the office! The office is always open when the church is open.*

I headed that way. Sure enough, there she was sitting at her desk! I was excited to finally find her. I let myself into the office and stayed there to talk to her the entire service. It was fun getting to know her better, and I loved watching her expressions and looking into her blue eyes.

As we were talking, I blurted out, "Nancy, you need to quit looking at me with those beautiful blue eyes. They make me just melt."

She looked away, not knowing what to say. I knew I had embarrassed her, but it was how I felt, and it kind of tickled me to see her reaction.

Just before midnight, as the night service came to an end, the ushers came in with the communion cups and the bread. We were watching the service on the television in the office and joined along as everyone took communion.

I said to Nancy, "This is significant. This is our first communion together, and she looked at me like "are you nuts?" But that was okay. I knew she didn't know what I knew.

The evening went by fast, and I felt encouraged because this time I went home with her phone number in my pocket!

***

Now heading to Ohio, I had put the number in my wallet so I wouldn't lose it. I would call her when I got settled. I didn't want to come across as pushy and scare her, but truthfully, I was very anxious to call her.

As soon as I arrived and got the fifth-wheel set up, I gave her a call. I was disappointed as it went to her voicemail. I felt like we had broken the ice, but it seemed like it was shaky ground. I could tell she enjoyed our conversation, but I also could sense that she was very cautious. I wondered if she would call me back, and if she didn't, what would be my next step?

Chapter Five
The Date

[Nancy]

Ray didn't call me right away, which was okay with me. New Year's Eve was on a Wednesday, and on Saturday, while I was pulling into the parking lot of Skateland to go roller skating with my kids, my phone rang. I looked down at my phone and said, "It's Ray Painter." My oldest daughter, Denise, was in the front seat, and Mary and Richie were in the back. They all at once said, "Answer it!"

"No way! Not with all of you listening."

The car was full, and they were all giggling thinking this was "cool!" It was like I had suddenly become a teenager. I did not want to talk with him while everyone was listening. It would be hard enough without my family listening to what might be a very awkward conversation. The kids were funny. I didn't understand why, but for some reason, they were excited about this.

We had a fun time skating and I decided to try not to think about talking with Ray until later. I was happy to be skating to the music with the kids and enjoying each other.

Ray had left me a voicemail to call him, so that night when everything was quiet, I returned his call. I was surprised at how easy it was to talk with him. When we were done talking, he said he would like to call me. I enjoyed our conversations. It was a "safe" way for me to get to know who he really was. I got glimpses into his heart and some of the walls were beginning to fall, just a little.

After we had talked a few nights, he told me he would be back home around Valentine's Day and would like to take me out to the Fireside Dinner Theatre. It's an upscale restaurant with different shows playing throughout the year. For Valentine's Day, it would be a '50s musical, perfect music for a fun night. During our conversations, he kept assuring me we would have fun, good fellowship, and great food. I was anxious about venturing out of my comfort zone. But in his voice I felt his confidence and was assured that he was right—It would be a wonderful time.

One night before going to bed, I noticed the clock. The time was 11:11. It got my attention, as God had used this number in the past to remind me that He was with me. I knew He was, but it helped me to be more aware that He was holding onto me through all the difficult times. I wondered why it appeared now, but I fell asleep peacefully, knowing that God had His arms around me and that I was his child.

The next morning, I awoke and headed off to work as usual. It was a busy day, but as I glanced at the clock, I noticed it was 11:11 a.m. It surprised me, but I was busy

and went on with my day. Then later, it showed up in some paperwork. You have to understand, I do not just sit at my desk, waiting for the clock to turn. I was busy, making copies, answering phones, and running down the hall on errands. This was something I could not cause to happen.
I went out to pick something up during my lunch hour and as I looked to check the time, it was 1:11 p.m. I laughed out loud and said to God, "What's up with this?" I remember feeling kind of amused and praying, "God, what are you up to now?"

That evening on my way home from work, my cell phone rang. It was Ray. He sounded happy.

"Hi! What are you doing?" he asked.

"I'm just on my way home from work. What are you up to?"

"I'm back in town and I'd like to see you."

My stomach did a flip-flop. Talking on the phone had become a time I always looked forward to, but I was not ready to meet him face to face! Then I remembered 11:11 and realized God was reassuring me that He was with me, and I didn't have to be afraid.

Ray asked if he could pick me up during my lunch hour the next day and take me out to eat. I was thankful he hadn't asked to see me right away. I needed some time to recover and talk to God about meeting this man face-to-face.

The next day I went to work and as the clock approached noon, I confided to my friend, "Margaret, I'm really nervous."

She looked at me with encouraging eyes and said, "Nancy, you are just going to lunch with a friend. It will be okay." I smiled and thanked her.

It wasn't long until Ray appeared at the office door with his big, contagious smile. He waited for me to join him and we walked outside to his car. He opened the car door for me, and I noticed he was wearing a cologne that had a masculine fragrance. It wasn't too strong, but it was pleasant and got my attention. I don't remember much about our conversation that day, but I really enjoyed our time together.

Another day he brought me his homemade tuna fish and noodle casserole, and we ate in the church café. It was delicious, but I noticed he loved salt and pepper, lots of pepper.

People at church were noticing us together. Everyone I worked with seemed happy and excited for me, maybe even more excited than me. Ray went back on the road, and it was a good time for me to really seek God. I felt I was falling for him, but I did not trust myself or my feelings. I had made too many mistakes already. Never again!

One Wednesday night, I was sitting in the back annex of the church worshipping. I enjoyed being there as it felt like my own private space with God. It was a time when I could let go of everything and enter into God's presence without distractions.

After church, I remembered I needed to go by the office. There, sitting in the chair at my desk, was Pastor Byrd. The volunteer office worker was busy in the back of the office. Pastor Byrd looked at me and said, "Nancy, I saw you during the service and God wants you to be enjoying what is happening in your life. You need to relax and trust God. I want you to say, 'I don't give a rip!'"

"What?"

"Just say it, Nancy!"

"Uhh, I don't give a rip?" I said hesitantly.

Pastor Byrd laughed his deep infectious laugh. It made me laugh, and I saw the office volunteer smiling.

"A little louder," Pastor Byrd said.

"I don't give a rip!" I guess it sounded a little more enthusiastic, but I still was unsure why I should say this.

When I got in my car away from everyone, I smiled, "I don't give a rip!" And then I shouted it a little louder! And louder! Soon I was laughing and even though that doesn't seem very "spiritual," something happened, and I relaxed a little more. I was stressed by this new relationship, but God knew I needed to laugh and put my trust in Him. God is so good!

Valentine's day was fast approaching. I started thinking about what to wear to the Fireside Dinner Theatre. It had been a long time since I had bought something new for a special occasion, so my daughter Denise and I decided to go shopping. It felt good to be able to share all the feelings and thoughts running rampant in my head with my daughter.

While we were in one of the stores, Denise said, "Mom, come here! I found a pretty top you might like for your date!" The words, "for your date" hit me like a rock. I felt sick to my stomach and a panicky feeling overtook me.

"I'm sorry, sweetheart. I can't look right now. Can we do it another time?" We had fun shopping and visiting, but

I couldn't bring myself to actually think about this big date. Denise was so supportive. We went another day and found a pretty dark blue top to go with a skirt I already had.

When the big night came, Denise came over to help me get ready and calm my nerves. To some of you, this probably sounds insane to be filled with so much fear. I don't totally understand it all either, but it was real.

My son-in-law, Tim, came by and jokingly said, "Are you going to let him kiss you?" He had no idea what happened to me when he said that. It hadn't even entered my mind! I had no clue what I would do and didn't want to even think about it.

Denise helped me decide on earrings and she helped me with my hair. She encouraged me and then left before Ray got there. It wasn't long before the doorbell rang. I opened the door and there he stood, dressed in a dark suit with a big smile on his face. He looked very handsome. I think strikingly handsome is more like it. He had gifts in his hands. We went to the kitchen table, and I opened the first gift bag and found a cute Valentine's dog.

"Press his foot." He was excited to give it to me, so I pressed the foot.

The dog panted, then barked and said, "Where's my hug? C'mon, give me a hug. Give me a hug. Ruff Ruff." It was cute and funny and made me laugh (I never realized he was hoping for a hug). He also bought me a corsage and a beautiful silver necklace with the initial "N" on it. I was overwhelmed, not expecting all of this!

He helped me with my coat and we headed on our way. I found it easy to talk with him in spite of my nervousness. When we got to the theater, it was cold, so he dropped me off at the door. When I got up to the door, there was a line to get inside. I had worn a thin coat because I didn't have a dressy winter coat, and the wind was penetrating my body. I was shivering! Soon he arrived and stood behind me to shelter me from the wind. It felt good to have someone looking after me. It had been a long time. He also commented several times about how beautiful he thought I looked.

When we went inside the restaurant, I found we were going to have a Valentine's Day picture taken. Then we were escorted to the dining area. It was a beautiful setting and they had placed us close to the fireplace and the piano. The music softly playing helped me to relax. The food was excellent, and the conversation flowed easily.

After our dinner, we went to the theatre section of the restaurant. The music was from the '50s and '60s and we knew every one of the songs! We found ourselves singing along with some of the songs. During a few of the songs, everyone would stand. When I looked at Ray standing next to me, even though there was no room as it was a theatre, he was dancing to the music. He was enjoying it so much; I couldn't help but laugh. He was so cute and enthusiastic. It was the most fun I can remember having in a long, long time. It was wonderful!

When we arrived home, he walked around, opened the car door for me, and walked me to the house. I unlocked the door and he came in. After I had put the leftover carton away and set my things down, he helped me off with my coat. As I was saying goodnight and thanking him for a wonderful evening, he drew me into his arms. I remember looking up into his eyes and I knew he was going to kiss me. Then he stopped. I looked at him, not sure what was happening. He said, "I really want to kiss you right now, but I feel the Lord said to wait." I felt a mixture of relief and disappointment. But I thought it was wonderful that he was listening to the Lord.

"Ray, I understand that, and it's fine with me. I think it's a good thing." I smiled at him, and I knew he knew that I meant it. I wanted our relationship to go slow. I didn't understand it, but for some reason, I felt safe with him.

Chapter Six
Big Steps

[Ray]

I was thankful I had gotten my fifth-wheel set up because the day after I arrived in Ohio, we had a lot of snow. I had a "polar pack" on my trailer, which was supposed to keep it from freezing up. Well, it froze up solid, so I couldn't use the shower. I had no running water at all in my trailer and it was not very comfortable. To shower, I had to walk through the snow to get to the public shower at the campground. I had all the heaters running to try to keep it warm. My campsite was right next to the lake and the wind was coming off the lake, so it was really cold!

But every night after work, I would get all settled, bundle up under the covers and call Nancy. I looked forward to our talks and the chance to get to know her better. I initially told her I would call her every few days, but it ended up being pretty much every night. We would share our day with each other, and I sensed that she was becoming more and more comfortable talking to me. One night I told her I had a devotional book that I read before going to sleep. I asked her if she'd like me to read it to her.

"Yes, I'd like that!"

And so, it became our routine, although one night while I was reading, she fell asleep.

"Nancy, are you there?"

"Oh, yes! I'm sorry. It was a long day and there's something about your voice that makes me feel comfortable and helps me relax."

I was thankful she didn't say I was boring her.

When I felt the time was right, I asked her to go out with me on Valentine's Day. I knew it was a big step, and I was happy when she agreed to go. I made reservations for us and decided to get the full package deal, including a picture and all. I knew it was going to be a memorable night.

Working at the power plant turned out to be a challenge. We had a young foreman, and I noticed he had made several mistakes but would try to cover them up. I felt like I needed to watch my back because if he messed up, he would probably try to blame someone else. It was not a good work environment and when I considered everything else that was happening, I eventually decided not to stay there. I went to the office offsite for what they call the "body count." There they put you through a machine that checks to see if you have radiation in your body or if you're contaminated before they give you an "all clear". I checked out fine, and they cut me my final check and I headed back to the campsite.

I packed up, hooked onto my fifth-wheel, and headed out. This time I was excited to go home. I knew I was going to get to see Nancy so I was pretty happy. I knew she was working, but I called her as soon as I knew she was off work. She was very surprised when I told her I was back and wanted to take her to lunch the next day, but she agreed to go. We were making progress!

I picked her up the next day at noon, and we had an hour together--not enough time, but Valentine's Day was just around the corner and we would have a real date.

Nancy didn't know about what the Lord had said to me and often I caught her off guard. But I was so confident. I was sure of what the Lord had said to me, and there was no doubt in my mind that Nancy was going to be my wife.

When the night of our big date arrived, I dressed up and headed to her home. When I rang the doorbell and she opened the door, she looked beautiful, and her sweet spirit touched my heart. Her home felt inviting and peaceful.

The drive to the Fireside went by fast. The dinner and atmosphere were everything I hoped they would be, and more. As we finished eating and were boxing up our leftovers, I impulsively wrote on the to-go boxes "RP" and "NP". I remember she looked at me kind of strangely, and she said something. I can't remember what it was, but I just said, "Don't worry about it. It'll be fine." It was a good time for us to head to the theatre. The music that night was great and her smiles and laughter showed me she was having a fun time too.

When I dropped her off at her house and was about to leave, she was so sweet and soft and tender. I really wanted to kiss her that night, and I pulled her into my arms. But when I went to kiss her, the Holy Spirit said, "No, now is not the time."

Okay, Lord. I stopped. I didn't kiss her.

There was another time I almost kissed her before the Lord said yes. We were sitting on the couch visiting and I felt drawn to her. I took off my glasses and leaned towards her, but just then her son Richie came home and walked into the living room. It seemed to be not very good timing, but actually, it was perfect. God says in His Word that with every temptation, He will make a way of escape. It's not that I wanted to escape kissing her. At the time it seemed like a very good idea, but more than that, I wanted to obey God. I believe what the Bible says—obedience is better than sacrifice,* and I certainly wanted to be in tune with the Lord at all times and let Him lead in our relationship.

While I was back home, I asked Nancy to go with me to the annual church business meeting. We sat together and were visiting with people after the meeting. I saw Pastor Ruben and went over to say hi to him. As we were talking, he shared with me what he felt God was saying to him. He told me that God said to tell me that I had been faithful and God was pleased. He also told me several times that it was okay for me to get married whenever I wanted. It was a confirmation that I was free to move forward, and it was surprising to me that it happened at a business meeting.

*I Samuel 15:22

Chapter Seven
He's Safe – And Fun!

[Nancy]

One Sunday night Ray came by to pick me up for the service at church. That night he told me of his plans to go to Bible school. He wanted to include me in his plan. He wanted me to go with him, which, of course, would mean marrying him and leaving everything. I couldn't imagine how this could happen. I told him I couldn't go with him unless I knew for sure this was God's plan. It would be a huge step of faith and the only way I would go with him was if God made it very clear. I told him that I had to know, not just 100%, but 110%! This would affect my children, my job, everything! I would not go without that confirmation.

That Sunday night Pastor Byrd preached a message about Abraham and his faith. How Abraham left his family and everything behind and went out to a place he didn't know. Ray and I both knew God was talking to me. I was weeping, and Ray asked me if I wanted to go forward in answer to the altar call to move in faith for God's plan in our lives. At first, I shook my head no, but my heart was saying yes. When I looked at Ray, he knew and took my hand. We walked forward, hand in hand, and said "yes" to whatever God had in store for us. This happened Sunday night, April 19th, 2009. I could have said "no", and stayed in my seat. It felt safer, but God is so good and helped me to move forward.

Monday morning when I got to church, Pastor Brad was standing by the mailboxes in the front of the office. He looked over my way and grinned, "Way to go, Nancy!" I couldn't figure out what he meant and I must have looked confused. "I loved that you walked forward to the altar in front of everyone holding Ray's hand." I thought, *oh my, I did do that in front of everyone*. I knew that we had probably surprised some people. But I knew that obeying God was more important than what other people thought, and I know Pastor Brad believed that too.

Not long after this, one of the younger pastors came into the office at work. He wanted to talk with one of the other pastors who was in a counseling session. He decided to wait around for a bit. We got talking and he asked me what was new in my life. I mentioned that Ray and I had started seeing each other. We talked a little, and then he said, "Nancy, I know that you have people who speak into your life, but I feel I need to say something. The word 'safe' keeps coming to me."

I was so amazed! I had told Denise and my friend Ann, that I felt safe with Ray and that I didn't understand why, but no one else knew how I was feeling. But God knew! He was the One who was telling me this was a safe relationship. I shared with him how I had felt the Lord was saying that to me too. We both laughed and he said, "That's the Holy Ghost!" He then gave me a high five, and we laughed some more.

I needed this confirmation, as God was pulling bricks from the wall I had built. He was gently directing me and I felt overwhelmed by his love and kindness.

One Saturday, Ray was over visiting, and my daughter Mary was going to go somewhere. I hugged her and she headed out. A minute later, we heard a crash. Somehow, she didn't see Ray's big, shiny, red Dodge one-ton dually truck in our driveway and backed into it. She came sheepishly walking through the door and apologized. Ray was very gracious, and thankfully, the damage wasn't much. He was so calm; it impressed me. I was beginning to fall for this guy. He had character.

I soon discovered another side of Ray....

One night we went out for supper and decided to stop at a pizza place. There were no other customers there at the time. As we walked up to the counter to decide what we wanted, he had his hand on my back and all of a sudden, he took the back of my bra strap and pulled it so it snapped on my back.

My mouth gaped open, "You can't do that!" I said, my eyes wide with disbelief.

"I just did." He grinned.

"I know! But that's just not right!"

He started laughing. He laughed so hard I wasn't sure what I should do. Ray had never done anything inappropriate. He was a perfect gentleman. He hadn't even kissed me yet. I thought it must be his way of having fun. Maybe he wanted to see my reaction or maybe it was a spur-of-the-moment impulse—I didn't know for sure—but there was no way I was letting on, that despite my initial shock, I was on the verge of laughing too. I mean what would this guy do next if I allowed such behavior?

His laughter was contagious, and I decided I better change the subject. I remember when he dropped me off, he got tickled all over again thinking about it, and I'm afraid I may have smiled a little.

Another night after we had been out, he came into the house and we sat on the couch and talked. Then out of the blue, he casually said, "Well, if you're not going to invite me into your bedroom, I'm going to leave now."

Without thinking, I reached over and backhanded him in the chest. With that, he just roared with laughter.

"No one has ever hit me before!"

"Well, it's about time somebody did!"

Again, he had shocked me, but this time I knew for sure it was done in fun with no wrong intentions. He was amused at my response and couldn't quit laughing. He couldn't believe I actually hit him. I surprised myself, but I explained to him that it was well deserved. In the end, I believe he agreed.

Talking over the phone, I had no idea that this side of Ray existed, but I had to admit, I really enjoyed our time together. He was fun and spontaneous. We shared serious conversations, but he was also light-hearted. He would say something and a grin would flash across his face, and I would realize he was joking. His laugh was deep and real. It would be hard to say goodbye when it was time for him to go back to work and leave for Pascal, Washington.

Chapter Eight
Going to the Chapel

[Ray]

I had planned to make the trip to Pascal, Washington in two days. The first day I drove until I got to Wyoming where I found a truck stop. It was night. There wasn't much there. It was kind of a desolate place. I backed into a slot and crawled into my fifth-wheel. I was so tired, I didn't open up any of the slide-outs, and just crawled up in the bed, but before going to sleep I wanted to talk to Nancy. I wanted to hear her voice. It was good to be able to share my day with her and then fall asleep.

The next morning, I got up and started on my way to Pascal. It was amazing as I was going through the Pipestone Mountains in Idaho. This was May and it was snowing! Yet, it was beautiful, and I was enjoying the drive until I had a breakdown in Montana. It was Sunday, and I was supposed to report to work on Monday. As I was coming down the mountains into a valley, I hit a bump and the spring on my fifth-wheel broke. I limped it into town, not knowing what I was going to do. I talked to a guy at the gas station and thankfully, there was a man in town who did repairs on fifth-wheels, and he put a new spring on it that day. He told me the spring had already been cracked and the bump just finished it.

I had to drive through the mountains and snow in Idaho. I was getting tired and had a long way to go. I called Nancy and we talked for a couple of hours. I knew she was tired too, but she stayed on the phone and helped me stay awake. I made it to Pascal that night and parked my fifth-wheel at a campground.

When I woke up, I noticed that it was beautiful and green because they watered it all the time. I was right next to the Yukon River, which was flowing hard out of the mountains. There were rapids by the park, and you could hear the water rustling and bouncing as it was coming down off of the mountains.

I left there to get my referral. Then I went through the process of getting started on the job. When I returned, I found I had some leaks in the water system because the pipes had frozen when I was in Cleveland, Ohio. I had to fix those.

While I was there, Nancy and I were talking every night. I missed her and wanted to get married as soon as we could. We went through several scenarios of having a wedding at the church in Rockford. It would be difficult to have a small wedding because together we had nine children plus grandchildren.

My son who is a pastor was trying to help and suggested we might consider going on a cruise, and he could marry us on the cruise ship. We thought about that because it sounded fun and exciting, but decided it wouldn't work. We were on a time frame to get to Bible college and it would take more time and planning than we really could afford. We each had a home that we would need to sell or rent while we were gone. There was so much to do!

Someone mentioned to me there was a chapel in Coeur D'Alene, Idaho. They told me that you could just get your license at the courthouse, walk across the street to the chapel, and get married. I thought, "Wow! That sounds pretty cool!"

I decided to talk with Nancy about it. I knew that it would be a big step for her to actually get on a plane by herself and fly up here, not knowing anyone around here or anything about where she'd be going! I wondered if she would be brave enough.

Chapter Nine
An I Really Doing This?

[Nancy]

While Ray was in Pascal, one Sunday at church, a lady I casually knew started talking to me. She was very nice, and I know she had good intentions. She had noticed that Ray and I had been seeing each other. She warned me that we were moving too fast. I had thought that myself, so I listened to her. She said he hadn't been widowed very long and that we should date for a lot longer, at least a year. Her heart was definitely in the right place, and I felt genuine concern. I left the church feeling very troubled and confused.

Ray called that night, and I told him what happened and that I thought she could be right. He said, "Let me ask you one thing. How did you feel before you talked with her?"

"I felt pretty peaceful."

"How do you feel now?"

"Confused."

"And where does confusion come from?" he questioned.

"From the enemy Satan," I answered. I knew the Bible verse that says, "For God is not the author of confusion but of peace..." (I Corinthians 14:33) I immediately felt at peace again. All the confusion left. Ray was right. Although right intentioned, this was not a conversation directed by God. It made sense, and usually, it is the right way to build a relationship, but it was not how God was leading us. I never had any other objections from friends or family. Everyone around me was excited and happy to see us together. It was like watching a love story unfold. Sometimes I felt like I was also watching, because God was the director, and I had to just follow His lead.

Ray assumed we were getting married, but he hadn't officially asked me. One day we were texting and I said, "You have never officially asked me to marry you, but you are making plans as if you had."

He texted back, "Will you marry me?"

I was at work and showed Margaret and we both chuckled. Even though it was not the most romantic proposal, it was very sincere. Of course, I replied, "Yes." Later, he sent me a picture of a ring he had bought. As you can tell, this was not a typical engagement.

There was so much to figure out! It was overwhelming! I had two teenagers to think of and couldn't just run off to Bible college unless God made a way for it to happen. They were my first priority. I felt God was moving that way, but how was that even possible?

My daughter Mary had told me she wanted to be on her own even before Ray came into my life, but she started making plans to move. She has always been my independent child. My emotions were all over the place, but her mind was made up. She had graduated from high school and was working and going to Rock Valley College. She wanted to make her own way in life. I had to let go of her, but it was difficult.

Without knowing that Ray wanted me to go to Rhema Bible College with him, my son Richie came to me one day and said he would like to spend his last year of high school with his sister Britney, her husband, and their children in Arizona. Richie is my adopted son and we had kept a strong relationship with his biological siblings, and I love them, but I was surprised that he wanted to go live there.

Richie had flown out to visit them during the summer break from school. They had told him they would like for him to stay with them for a while. I asked him if this was something that he was sure he wanted to do. It would be a big change. He was sure.

It seemed God was making the path clear. To tell the truth, some of this is a blur, as there was so much happening at one time. Mary was making plans to move, and Richie was planning to live in Arizona. I didn't take notes of everything or write in a journal. I wish I had, but life was moving very fast! Without God's direction and help, this was impossible. We would need to be at Bible school in September, just a few months away!

One day while I was working at the church, Ray called. He was excited because he had found a place in Coeur d'Alene, Idaho called the Hitching Post Wedding Chapel. We had talked about eloping, and Ray felt this would be the perfect place to do it. We could get our marriage license and walk across the street to this little western chapel and be married by a minister on the same day. He told me to look it up on the internet and see what I thought.

I told Kellie and Margaret, and Kellie went right to her computer and found it. It looked perfect! It was a beautiful small chapel where we could be married by a minister and not a Justice of the Peace. During WWII, Farragut Naval Training Center was located a few miles away from this chapel, and couples would line up at the door to get married before their spouse would be shipped off to war.

Ray's idea was for me to fly out to Pascal, Washington. Then the next day we could drive over to Idaho (which was only about a two-and-a-half-hour drive) to be married!

On our honeymoon, we would drive his fifth-wheel back to Illinois, stopping by Yellowstone Park, Glacier National Park, and anywhere else we thought would be fun. Wow! This was getting exciting, but also scary! It was becoming real. It would be a plunge into a whole new life and my faith sometimes would waver. After all, I had grown comfortable and happy with my life. I needed to pray...we needed to pray together!

We did pray, and it seemed right. There was peace in it. Shortly after that while I was working, I was walking down the hall and, in the middle of all the Christian music that normally played through the intercom, I heard the song "Going to the Chapel". It was an old song, and I knew the words. In my head, I started singing along and smiling.

Wow! What an amazing God who keeps leading me step by step, helping me to overcome my fears. He is so good!

It came time to take Richie to the airport to go to his sister and brother-in-law's home in Arizona. He packed everything he could and brought his guitar as a carry-on. He gave one of his friends some of his games, his television, and some other things he knew his friend would enjoy. Richie has always had a generous heart. It was very hard to take him to the airport. Thankfully, it was only a short drive from Winnebago to the Rockford airport—I knew saying goodbye would be difficult.

We hugged and I watched as he walked away. My heart was sad as I drove back home alone. I know he had to be feeling emotions over this huge transition, but he did seem happy and excited.

Mary moved out shortly after that and took our family dog, Shadow, with her. I was thankful that she would have Shadow with her to watch out for her. Her leaving was very difficult for me. She had always been my "baby girl." I felt protective.

When I would talk with her, she would say, "Mom, I'm doing this because I want to be independent and on my own." Her mind was made up and she has always been a very determined young woman. Most of the time, her independent spirit has been a good thing coupled with her very tender heart. At times I wondered if she was doing this because Ray had entered my life, but she always assured me that was not the case.

Ray and I were talking every night. We decided to set the date of June 3rd as the day to get married. His job would be ending in Pascal, and we could marry and leave in the fifth-wheel on our honeymoon. Ray bought me a ticket and the plan was that I would fly out on the day before the wedding. He would pick me up at the airport and we would go to a western store and buy our wedding outfits.

"Don't buy a dress," he said, "It's the Hitching Post. We will dress western and pick something out when you get here." It sounded like a fun idea, and it freed me from having to decide what to wear.

Everyone at work was understanding and supportive. They were so happy for us.

***

Before I knew it, the morning of June 2nd arrived!

I was awake even before the alarm went off. I rubbed my eyes and looked around. It was still dark, and before my eyes could even adjust, I felt both excitement and fear overwhelming me.

Am I really doing this? The answer came back as quickly as the question.

Yes, I am! There was the proof—next to my bed lay my burgundy suitcase all packed except for a few items I needed for my morning routine. This was real! I had not been dreaming! In the darkness of the room, I sat up. No one was there to talk with me, not even Shadow, who had always seemed to understand. My emotions started to battle, each one wanting to rule.

Fear started to grab hold of me. *What are you doing? Are you sure you are following God? You know you're not enough. You'll never measure up.*

I began to pray. "God help me!" His peace began to fill me. Whatever lay ahead, I knew God was involved and leading me. There were times that fear would try to grip my heart, but I was getting good at recognizing it and had become adept at shutting it down. I believed in this decision. I had prayed and the answer was clear, but it was still a big step of faith. I inhaled deeply and threw the covers back. I needed to get going. I wanted so much to look beautiful today! Again, I whispered, "God help me." as I began to get ready. It seemed that prayer had become like breathing to me.

It wasn't long until the doorbell rang, and there was my friend, Cindy. She was right on time, actually a little early. Cindy had volunteered to drive me to the bus station that would take me to O'Hare Airport. When I opened the door, I was met with her bright smile. She was happy for me and so encouraging.

I locked up the house and she helped me carry my luggage down the steps to her car. We decided to stop for coffee as we headed out to the bus station. As we chatted, the aroma of fresh hot coffee and the presence of a good friend were comforting to me. It felt good not to be alone. We sipped our coffee and visited, but in no time, we were there! Cindy gave me a big hug goodbye, and again I was on my own.

As I settled into my bus seat, thoughts of the path that brought me to this day began to flood my mind. I thought about all I was leaving behind and the unknown that was ahead. I silently talked with God as we traveled. Ray had texted me. It seemed he always knew the right thing to say, and I felt encouraged. We would talk when I got to the airport.

Everything went smoothly, and soon I was on the flight to Pascal. I had a window seat and I loved the view from above. We climbed above the clouds and the sun was shining. The skies were blue. God was taking me on another adventure. Although I'm normally not an adventurous person by nature, I felt excited knowing God was with me and holding my hand.

As we came close to Pascal, I could see small circles of green below with what looked brown all around them. *What is that?* I wondered. Finally, I decided to ask the man next to me if he knew. He told me we were above a desert area and the green dots were areas that were watered, probably for some kind of crop.

When it was time for the plane to land, I freshened my face as my stomach did flip-flops. Soon I would see Ray.

I wondered what he was thinking. He'd always been so sure. Was he sure now? *I guess I will soon find out.*

The plane landed and I grabbed my purse and carry-on bag and headed toward the exit. As I walked off the plane and looked around, there stood Ray. He looked confident and strong and he had a huge smile on his face as I walked toward him. My stomach was still in turmoil, but his eyes reassured me. This was the right path for us. He took my carry-on bag and looked down at me.

"I'm so proud of you," he said.

"I don't understand. Why?"

"It took a strong woman of faith to do what you've just done—to get on that plane and fly out here!"

"Well, I've been pretty nervous about it all." With that, he wrapped his arms around me and gave me a big hug.

Chapter Ten
Tomorrow's Our Day

[Ray]

I was excited when it was time to pick Nancy up from the airport and finally see her again. I will never forget that look on her face as I watched her come walking through the turnstile. She looked just beautiful, and I was so happy to see her.

As she walked towards me, I could tell she needed some reassurance. I had no doubts that this was God's plan. I hugged her close for a moment and asked her about her flight. Then I realized we needed to get going.

"Let's go get the rest of your luggage. We need to get to the Ranch King Store before they close. Tomorrow's our wedding day!" I took her hand as we headed to the baggage carousel center, grabbed her luggage, and headed to the truck.

As I opened the door for her and helped her up into the truck, I could see in her eyes that she appreciated my care for her. She was a treasure to me, and I wanted her to know it.

It was a short drive to the store in Kennewick, but I had no idea how long it would take to pick out our wedding outfits, so I wanted to get there and have plenty of time.

Nancy had never been in a western store before, but we were getting married at the Hitching Post, so I figured western wear would be appropriate. I had fun shopping with her.

After looking around some, I hollered, "Hey Nancy, we need cowboy hats!"

"Really?" She looked surprised.

"Yes, for sure! It's not western until you have the hats!"

After trying on a few, some of which looked comical, we found some matching ones that we both liked. Next on the list were cowboy boots. Nancy looked shocked at how expensive they were, but I insisted we needed them too. She found a shiny brown leather pair and tried them on.

I had never seen her in anything like that. She looked cute as she walked around trying them on.

"Maybe now I could even wrestle down a calf!" she laughed. I could tell she was enjoying this too.

We managed to complete our outfits before closing time and then headed out for dinner. Dinner went by fast, as we had a lot to catch up on and were excited about our wedding day.

After dinner, it was time to head to the fifth-wheel. I felt a little awkward, and I could tell Nancy was too. I'm not sure why, maybe because we knew we were in close quarters with one bedroom. I knew she trusted me, and we were both committed to doing this the right way.

We talked a while about the plans for our wedding day, and then I told her that the bedroom would be hers tonight, and I would take the couch.

"Ray, you're too tall—that won't be comfortable for you, and I don't mind sleeping on the couch." The couch was a sofa sleeper and I started to pull it out, but she said it wasn't necessary as there was plenty of room for her. I finally agreed and brought her a pillow and a blanket. I hugged her and went off to bed.

Chapter Eleven
I Do!

[Nancy]

After Ray went off to bed, I lay there on the couch trying to go to sleep. I could hear his steady breathing in the next room and knew he was sound asleep. It wasn't as easy for me to fall asleep, and just as I started to doze off, the fan above me started squeaking!

Oh, no! I'll just ignore it.

But it seemed it just got louder and louder. Finally, I decided I had to do something! I got up and stumbled around in the dark looking for the switch. I found a switch plate with several switches. The first one I turned on lit up the whole room, so I quickly turned it off. There was only a small partition between the front room and the bedroom and I did not want to wake Ray. The next one didn't seem to do anything, so I turned it off quickly. Finally, I tried a switch and suddenly I heard a grating loud noise as the bedroom slide-out started to close.

I quickly shut it off and heard, "Nancy.... what are you doing? My bed is moving." It took everything I had to keep from laughing out loud. I pictured him sleeping peacefully one moment and then abruptly feeling the bed begin to move and shake!

Maybe he is wondering what he is getting into now, I giggled. But I did not want to wake him. I was trying to be quiet!

"I'm sorry, Ray. I was trying to turn off the fan without waking you. It's squeaking."

He came out and saw my sheepish grin.

"It's okay," he smiled. Then he showed me where the switches were and what they were for. He was so sweet about it. He slid his bed back out and went back to go to sleep. Eventually, I drifted off too, and when I woke up, it was our wedding day!

In the morning, we had a quick breakfast and headed out to Coeur D'Alene, Idaho. As we neared Spokane, the desert area opened up, and the barren area turned green with a beautiful river flowing alongside the road.

We found the courthouse without any problem. There was no line at the office when we got there, and we quickly filled out the paperwork. Ray paid the license fee and we started to walk across to the chapel.

Everything moved so quickly at the courthouse. I had to stop! My heart was pounding! *Is this really happening? Whoa!*

"Ray, can we stop for a minute?"

"Sure. We can sit on that bench." He was holding my hand as we walked over and sat down.

"Ray, are you 100% sure we are doing the right thing?"

"Yes, I am. No doubts."

"We are doing everything very fast. Our children aren't here. It's not too late to change our minds."

"Nancy, I know, and I think you do too, that this is God directing our footsteps. I am so sure that all we have to do is walk it out. He wrapped his arm around me, and we sat on the bench for a few minutes longer. My heart settled and he took my hand as we walked over to the chapel.

When we arrived, we were met by the pastor. We liked him right away. He showed us the various rooms where we could say our vows. They were all charming, some bigger than others, with gorgeous flower arrangements. We picked a small, simple chapel, but it was beautifully decorated. Then he showed us each a room where we could change into our outfits.

When I came out, Ray was standing there waiting. He looked strikingly handsome in his cowboy outfit—hat, boots, and all. It seemed a little funny for me to be dressed in western gear on my wedding day. I even had on a new western belt with a buckle he had bought for me. I hoped he thought I looked pretty, even though it was not the normal dress for a wedding. Again, I felt assured as I looked into his eyes.

We went into the room and the pastor began the ceremony. His words reflected our hearts. As he moved through the ceremony, all of the vows were perfect. We were giving ourselves to each other and making a commitment to Christ to love and honor one another.

I had often wondered how I would ever feel comfortable with Ray kissing me for the first time at our wedding in front of what I thought would be a group of family and friends. I had no idea what to expect, but I knew we were waiting on the first kiss until this day.

After we looked into each other's eyes and said our vows, the pastor said, "you may kiss the bride." The pastor immediately left the room. Ray took me in his arms and kissed me. His kiss was warm and tender, yet confident and strong. Ray says that I melted in his arms and I know it's true.

It seems this is a good place to end our story, with a kiss and the promise of a new life together. It's where most romance stories end, yet it was just the beginning of a new life together with many ups and downs and adventures ahead.

Epilogue

[Nancy]

We went on our honeymoon and then to Rhema Bible College. We have been on so many adventures. We have had our disagreements, but I have never felt so loved and cherished. When we have had disagreements or times when we didn't understand each other, we both knew that God planned for us to be together and that there is always a solution when we ask for His help.

During one of our first misunderstandings, I went into the bedroom. Ray followed me. He sat down next to me on the bed.

"Nancy, I want you to say, "There's nothing wrong with Nancy."

"What! I can't say that. It's not true." I felt that if we had any problem, it was because I was defective in some way. It seemed strange that he wanted me to say this. I didn't understand. Ray would not leave me alone, so I tried to say it, but I couldn't. I believe it was what the Bible refers to as a "stronghold" in my life, a lie that Satan had planted and had taken root.

I asked Ray, "Can you say, 'There's nothing wrong with Ray?'" He easily said it.

"Well, I can't say that there's nothing wrong with me because it's not true! Will you just leave me alone for now?" I pleaded.

"No, I won't leave until you say it."

I was starting to feel angry as I physically could not say it, even when I tried. He started to pray for me. He prayed in the Spirit. Finally, as I tried, I was able to whisper it. He said, "Keep saying it." And I was able to say it louder. Over the next few days, Ray would ask me to say it again and soon it was not hard at all! I didn't realize it, but I was being set free. Free from a lie!

Weeks later, Ray was irritated with me over something and said, "What's the matter with you?"

I replied, "There's nothing wrong with Nancy!" And we both laughed.

I've seen this saying somewhere and it's true for us— *Of all the love stories I have heard, I love ours the best.*

But every love story is unique. God has an original plan just for YOU!

We wrote this story to let others know that no matter what you have been through, there is always hope with God. We didn't share all the details and hurt of losing a spouse through death or divorce, but if you have experienced it, you know the devastation.

Maybe you're still waiting for real love in your life. May I challenge you to put your hope in Jesus? He has the truest and most real love there is to be found.

If you surrender to Him and his plan for your life, you can be sure that all of His stories are filled with His incredible love for you. I promise you, it may not always be easy, but it will be an exciting journey.

I once read that if you want God to write your story, you must quit taking away the pen. It involves faith and trust in knowing God loves you and His plans for you are good! (Jeremiah 29:11)

May our story inspire you to follow Him closely in faith knowing that the best is yet to come!

Ray & Nancy

If you have never asked Jesus into your heart to be your Savior and Lord and would like to, please turn to the back of this book, page 268.

Part Two

True Stories of
Life and Love with Devotionals

By Nancy Painter unless otherwise indicated

These are 30 true stories of God showing up in our lives in many unique and personal ways to reveal His love and guidance.

Each story has a devotional and prayer to encourage and uplift you. These could be used for personal or group Bible studies. For a free 6-week group study guide, visit www.whataboutnancy.com.

Adventure Awaits

Are you an adventurous person? Are you willing to stand in long lines on a sweltering summer day to ride a roller coaster? Do you love to feel your stomach turn somersaults and scream at the top of your lungs, as the coaster plunges to the bottom and then climbs the next hill? Have you always longed to parachute from a plane and feel the wind blowing you everywhere as you plummet to the ground?

My husband, Ray, loves to go coyote hunting. On cold, snowy nights, he and his son will bundle up in their camouflage gear, grab their guns, and head out in the dark to wait patiently for a coyote to cross their sights.

While I love to stay at home on cold, snowy days, and cook soup, bundled up in a blanket with a book, Ray loves to get out and go somewhere—anywhere! He enjoys taking me along on his adventures (which, I have to admit, often end up being fun). For him, there is an excitement and challenge in braving the weather.

Although coyote hunting and parachute jumping are a little too exciting for my cautious personality, I have had many adventures in my life. When I was in my twenties, I moved away from my family and friends in Illinois to sunny California, where my good friend Donna was living, to start a new life. The freeways were, in themselves, quite an adventure!

Once I went white-water rafting. I'm not sure why I wanted to do this so much, but I guess we all long for some excitement in our life. Many years ago, when it was popular, I wallpapered our bathroom. This is an adventure I never plan on repeating.

And in 2009, I flew to Washington state to marry my husband, Ray. We then moved to Oklahoma to attend Rhema Bible College and traveled and lived in a fifth-wheel. After we were married, I discovered that I loved riding on the back of his Harley, exploring different places in this grand country of ours.

But the greatest adventure of my life has been in following Jesus. Maybe that sounds strange to you. I know many people think that being a Christian is boring and basically just a list of dos and don'ts. But real Christianity is not about religion, it is a relationship with the Person of Jesus Christ. He is never boring! He has taken me places where I would never have dreamed of going and surprised me in ways that I could never have thought possible. He is the author of creativity and adventure! He has never left me through all of these times.

Thank you for joining me on this book adventure. My prayer is that all of the stories will encourage you and help you to believe, not only in God but in whom He has created you to be.

DIGGING DEEPER

1. Do you tend to look at life here on earth as an adventure? A roller coaster that you're just surviving? Or a journey of changes with ups and downs that are to be expected?

2. How do you view your walk with Jesus? As a religious duty? As an exciting adventure? A little boring?

3. Complete joy, unending pleasure, and life are spoken of in Psalm 16:11. What is the main theme in this verse?

PRAYER

Lord, remind me to fully celebrate all the good in my life and give you thanks for every blessing. Teach me to cling to you during the hard days too, knowing that you are my rock and fortress even in uncharted territory. In faith, I move forward into the adventure of life today! Fill me with inspiration and enthusiasm for the life you have given me!

AMEN

A Lesson in Grace

My son Joe is kind, creative, sincere, and has a great sense of humor. I'm sure he would like me to add that he's pretty good-looking too, and it's true, he is. He's also quiet, but when you get him in a small group, he's so much fun! He always has me cracking up over something, often at myself, which is a good thing.

He wears several "hats" — he's a husband, a father to two beautiful girls, a chef, a manager, and an artist. When he was young, we jokingly called him, "joe-chef" instead of Joseph, because he loved to cook.

Melanie, Raedyn, Alex and Joe

After Joe was born, we found that our small home in Loves Park was feeling a little bit crowded. My sister, Patty, told us about a larger two-story home that was for sale on the same block where they were living. It was an older neighborhood in a nice area, and we decided to check it out. We loved the big rooms, and it had character that you don't always find in newer homes. It even had a big claw-foot bathtub, which we all loved for taking bubble baths. I miss that tub! The kids looked so cute in it with bubbles everywhere.

Because our home was older and drafty, often on cold mornings, Denise and "Joey" (his nickname growing up), would wrap their blankets around themselves and lay on top of the big floor register while I prepared breakfast. It's a "picture memory" that I love.

My sister and her family, my grandmother, and my great-aunt all lived on the same block. It was a great place to live, and our children ran back and forth playing together with their cousins. My grandmother, "Nana," enjoyed her grandchildren and great-grandchildren living so close. We have lots of good memories from that time.

Shortly after moving into our new home, Joey came in from playing and presented me with a bouquet of flowers. When I asked where he had gotten such beautiful flowers, he replied with a smile, "From all around our new neighborhood, mom!" Of course, we would have to have a talk about what belonged to us and what was our neighbor's, but looking down into his expectant eyes, I knew now was not that time. The lesson would come a little later, a big hug and a "thank you" was what I wanted to bestow on that smiling face right now. Such a sweet and tender heart! There would be a time to talk later.

One morning as Joey was rushing out the door to catch the bus for kindergarten, he stopped in the doorway to hug me goodbye. Then he looked up at me with a worried look on his face. "Mom, what day is tomorrow?" His voice was filled with concern.

"Well, tomorrow is the day after today,"

"Phew!" he answered, "I was worried 'cause my teacher said I had to have my paper back by tomorrow!" With that, he ran out the door to the waiting bus. I wanted to grab him and explain, but it was too late. I knew the teacher would enlighten him, but my heart hurt thinking I had given him the wrong explanation. He was in for a disappointment.

He was a busy little boy and in spite of all the creativity bottled up in this little guy, he did not enjoy his piano lessons. He had too many other things he wanted to do, like riding his big wheel up and down the block, playing ball, and exploring. His piano teacher, Mr. Ashley was starting to get frustrated with him.

Mr. Ashley came every week at the same time. He was giving Joey a lesson one day, when I overheard him say, "You are not practicing, Joey! Your parents are paying me every week and you are not doing your part! If you are not going to practice, you shouldn't be taking the lessons."

This was pretty harsh for Mr. Ashley! He was a quiet and kind man.

The week rolled by fast. I reminded Joey to practice, but he put it off until the day came for his lesson. When I mentioned Mr. Ashley would be coming, he panicked. "Oh mom," he said, "I haven't practiced. I'm going to be in a bunch of trouble."

"Yes, I think you are," I replied.

"Mom, I'm going to pray that he doesn't come today,"

"Well, I guess you can pray if you'd like," I said. But I was thinking, *that's not going to work.* And so, he prayed.

The time came for lessons, but Mr. Ashley did not show up. I thought this was strange as he was very punctual and reliable.

Joey practiced quite a bit the next week and was ready for his lesson when his teacher arrived at our home.

I welcomed Mr. Ashley at the door and told him we had missed him the week before. He looked at me confused and said, "Why, for

> God is so much more gracious and loving than we are!
>
> We don't always get what we deserve!

some reason, I thought you had told me not to come for lessons last week. I'm sorry if I misunderstood."

"Oh, that's okay," I smiled. "Come on in."

I called for Joey, and he and Mr. Ashley went into the dining room, to begin their piano lesson. I sat down at the kitchen table, thinking about what had just transpired.

As I sat there, the realization of what had happened began to flood my mind and heart. God had answered Joey's prayer! I had my way of thinking, which was he should be "chewed out". He hasn't done what he should have done.

That day God showed me something new. God is so much more gracious and loving than we are! We don't always get what we deserve! I'm so thankful for that because many times I have fallen short. I haven't done what I should have done!

The story of the prodigal son is an example of how when we turn our backs on the Father and squander everything, He's still waiting for us to come back with open arms to wrap around us. He places a clean robe on us and throws a party to celebrate that we are home! That's amazing! Wow! It's hard to understand that kind of love and forgiveness.

I learned so much from my children! Oh, to have child-like faith in His love! I grew up thinking God was watching me, and I better not mess up! But God gave me glimpses into His character and His love through my children. I came to know God, not as some far-off, detached entity watching me with a critical eye, but as my rescuer and my daddy who loves and cares for me. He has unconditional love for me. It is not based on my performance, but on who God is. The Bible says God is Love! He believes in me, even when I have trouble believing in myself. He will help me through all the situations in life if I will just put my trust in Him and ask Him for the help I need.

So as Joey took his piano lesson that day and I sat at my kitchen table, God taught me a lesson I will never forget. It was a lesson in His amazing grace!

DIGGING DEEPER

Hebrews 4:16 admonishes us, "Let us therefore come boldly to the throne of grace, that we may obtain mercy and find grace to help in time of need."

1. Why do you think we are to approach God with boldness and confidence?

2. In your time of need, have you ever felt it was difficult to approach God with confidence? Why or why not?

3. Think about the story of the prodigal son in Luke 15: 11-32. Whom do you identify with most—the father, the prodigal son, or the older brother?

PRAYER

Gracious Heavenly Father, help me to fully receive, feel and know the amazing grace that you extend to me as your child. Help me, day by day, to grow in awareness of your undeserved kindness, love, and mercy so that I can humbly offer grace to those around me to point them to the love of Christ Jesus.

AMEN

A Lesson in Trust

"Mommy, do we have to go to the doctor today?"
"Yes, honey, we'd better hurry and get ready. We don't want to be late."

It's a beautiful, sunny day, but I feel a little nervous. I'm almost certain my little girl has a plantar wart on her foot. I know that's nothing to worry about, no big deal, right? But Denise is just five years old, and to have a shot in her foot and then have a wart cut out is kind of scary, for her and for me. Her beautiful hazel eyes are so full of trust as she takes my hand to leave. I feel responsible.

"We'll take Joey to Aunt Patty's on the way, okay?"

"What's the doctor going to do for my foot, mommy?"

"Well, first the doctor will look at it. If it is a plantar wart, they'll have to take it off your foot.

"Will it hurt?"

"Well, it will probably hurt a little, but if they don't take it out now, you'll get more warts, and other people can catch them from you."

After dropping off Joey at Aunt Patty's, we head to the doctor's office. Denise is quiet. That's unusual for my little "chatter-box." I wonder what she's thinking, but I think I know.

"Here we are, honey," I inform her.

As we get out of the car, usually I say, "It's a parking lot; hold my hand." But today  it's not necessary. Her hand is in mine before I can even mention it. I ache a little for her. Part of me wants to rush her back home where it's safe, but I'm a grown-up now. I have to be sensible. As we wait in the lobby for our name to be called, we thumb through magazines and read stories, hoping to occupy our minds with something else. Finally, the nurse calls, "Denise Hunt."

Inside the doctor's office, the nurse asks Denise to take off her shoes and socks. After a short while, the doctor comes in to look at her foot. Yes, it is a plantar wart, and yes, it will have to be removed. The doctor explains to Denise that she will give her a shot so that it won't hurt as much, and then she leaves.

"Denise, do you want to pray with me before the doctor comes back?" I ask.

"Yes, mommy."

"Dear Jesus, Denise is afraid right now. We ask you to help her to be brave, and we ask that you will make it not hurt very much. In Jesus' Name. Amen."

Just as we finish, the doctor comes in and asks Denise to lie down. But as she starts to lie down, she sees the needle in the doctor's hand and panics.

Lord, please help her, I silently pray. But she's crying and won't lie still. *Lord, please!* my heart prays.

The doctor tells me I will have to try and hold her still. She's struggling and crying, and I'm trying to calm her. It's useless. She won't be calmed down. The doctor can hardly manage and when it's over, tells us she doesn't know if she removed the wart completely. She instructs us to make another appointment in a week and she will check it again.

I was a new Christian at this time and had only been born-again for about a year. As we drove home, questions kept popping into my mind.

Lord, why didn't you help her? She was so scared. She trusts you, and she trusts me. What do I tell her now? I don't understand. Help me to understand.

Denise interrupts my thoughts, "I'm sorry for everything, mommy."

"It's okay, honey. Come sit by me. She slides over, and I wrap my arm around her. I have no words.

"Do we have to go back?"

"Yes, we do, but if the wart is gone, the doctor won't have to do anything more. Let's not worry about it now, okay?"

The week goes by much too fast, and it's time to return to the doctor. We're back in the same office, and the doctor is looking at her foot.

Lord, please make the wart be completely gone, I pray silently.

"I'm sorry, Denise, but we didn't get it all," the doctor informs us.

My stomach sinks. *Not again, Lord. Should I ask her to pray with me again? Will He fail us again?* I decide to ask Denise. The doctor leaves for a moment.

"Denise, do you feel like you want to pray again?" I ask hesitantly.

"Yes, Mommy."

"Dear Jesus, we just pray that you will help Denise. Help her not to be afraid and help her to be brave. We ask that you make it not hurt. In Jesus' Name. Amen."

The doctor comes in and asks Denise to lie down. She does. She is still. The doctor removes the wart. Denise is holding my hand, but not crying!

Lord, what's different? What's happening? I don't understand this at all.

The doctor bandages her foot and we leave. As we get into the car to go home, Denise asks me to pray with her.

"Sure, honey," I reply.

And she prays, "Dear Jesus, I'm sorry I wouldn't be still the first time we were here. I wouldn't listen to you and believe you would help me. Thank you that it didn't hurt when I was still and listened to you. In Jesus' Name. Amen."

There are tears in her eyes and mine. That's it! It wasn't God's fault. He didn't fail us! He is always there! We just aren't being still and listening. We don't trust. We don't believe. Denise understood it so easily, and yet, I had to have her show me.

Thank you, Jesus! Thank you for teaching me through my little daughter. I will try to trust you more and listen and be still.

I guess as grown-ups, we sometimes would like to blame God for everything—for all the hurt and pain in the world. We may wonder, *Why does he let this happen to me?*

We don't always realize that He loves us so much that He gives us our freedom—freedom to choose Him or refuse His love. Freedom to follow Him or to go our own way. Freedom to trust Him or to trust only ourselves.

Children see things simply. They know what it means to trust and what it means to love. They have questions, but they also have faith.

DIGGING DEEPER

Read Mark 10:13-16

1. Why do you think that it's important to God that we have childlike faith?

2. What experiences in your life have taught you that God can be trusted?

3. In verse 14, Jesus says that the Kingdom of God belongs to those who are like these children. What does Romans 14:17 say about the Kingdom of God?

PRAYER

Lord, help me to use my intelligence. I know it is a gift from You and very much needed in the world today. But don't let me feel that I'm so smart that I need only rely on myself. Help me to use wisdom and have childlike faith to trust you for the answers that I need.

AMEN

Angel With a Chainsaw

I t was a beautiful, sunny Saturday morning when I walked out into my backyard. As I stood there, I could see the street that bordered the end of our three-quarters-acre lot. I watched as families drove by in their cars with their windows down. I could hear music playing from a distance, and it seemed everyone was excited for the Labor Day weekend.

I turned my eyes back to our yard and took a deep breath as I surveyed the obstacle before me. There it lay like a giant monster, challenging me. A huge branch had fallen from our willow tree from a storm that had gone through a few days earlier. The branch was the size of a tree!

I had no idea what I should do. My husband of twenty-four years was gone. I had relied on him, and now it was all up to me. It seemed as if a cloud of sorrow hung over me like the *Charlie Brown* character, *Pig-Pen,* who had a cloud of dust and dirt surrounding him. Some days were getting better. Yet, there were days like today, which normally would have been filled with family and fun, that seemed overwhelming to me.

I headed to the garage. I decided something had to be done and I was the one who had to do it! I needed a saw, but I wasn't even sure where to look, as the garage had never been my territory. Finally, after scrounging around, I found one. It was a pitiful, little thing, but it would have to do. It was all I had.

Thinking back, I must have looked pretty silly, armed with my 18-inch skinny weapon, climbing up on the limb of this huge branch, ready to conquer the giant! As I began to saw, I realized the blade was dull, extremely dull! I was frustrated. But then I remembered a Bible verse I had read, and I prayed out loud. "Lord, you said if the axe is dull, it takes a lot of strength. I could sure use some help!" (Ecclesiastes 10:10)

The words were barely out of my mouth, and I heard a voice behind me say, "Excuse me, ma'am, could I give you a few minutes of my time?" I was startled because we lived on a quiet cul-de-sac and I had not heard anyone drive

up our road or walk into our yard.

I turned to look and there stood an elderly man, dressed in blue jeans and a work shirt. *I hope he's not selling anything, but that's a strange way to phrase his question.* I climbed down off of the branch, and he explained that he wanted to cut the branch up for me.

"I really don't have any money, but maybe I could pay you something next Friday," I responded.

"I don't want to be paid. I only want to help you."

He walked to his truck parked on the cul-de-sac and came back carrying a huge chainsaw. He dove right into the task, and I was amazed at how fast he worked!

I decided to start a fire and pull the branches away as he cut them up. The willow burned quickly. All that was left was a few large logs, which I told him I could save for a campfire later.

While we worked and chatted, I thought how strange it was that I never heard him pull up in his truck or walk into our yard and that he appeared immediately after I prayed. Even though he was an elderly man, he worked with speed and strength which amazed me. I thanked him for his kindness and he was on his way. I never saw him again.

I shared what had happened with a few of my family and friends. My sister suggested that it may have been an angel, and as soon as she said this, I knew it was true! I remembered the Bible verse that says we may entertain angels unaware. (Hebrews 13:2)

But whether this was truly an angel or just a man, my God showed up to take care of me! My day got better and some of the sunshine made it through that dark cloud that engulfed me and into my heart!

DIGGING DEEPER

When we are in a desperate situation or feeling overwhelmed by our circumstances, the Bible is a source of light, hope, and truth that can encourage and uplift our spirits when our minds and emotions are clouding our view.

Below are some verses that may encourage you. Look up each one and write down what the verse is saying to you as you read and meditate on it. (Sometimes it's helpful to look up different Bible translations to gain a deeper understanding.)

- Psalms 34:18

- Psalms 37:5

- Psalms 91:15

- Isaiah 43:2

- Hebrews 4:12

- Hebrews13:5

There is a saying that God often works in mysterious ways. Have you ever experienced a time when, like Nancy, God helped you in an unexpected way or brought help through an unexpected person?

PRAYER

Lord, I don't want to limit you with unbelief or thinking that my prayers should be answered in a specific way. You are a limitless God with limitless resources, so help me, Lord, to trust you so deeply that whatever way you choose to work in my life is okay with me! Make your Word alive to me so that when I read it, I can see all the ways that you are speaking to me. When things are going well in life, help me to remember to thank you and be grateful for your many blessings, and when things feel out of control and hopeless, help me to remember that in you there is always hope and that you are in control.

AMEN

Are You Waiting for the Other Shoe to Drop?

When I was younger, I found that in times of happiness, I would sometimes feel a dread come over me. It was like I was "waiting for the other shoe to drop." I expected something to go wrong. I was just too happy. Something bad was just around the corner. I have no idea why I felt that way. Maybe I'm not alone in this. Have you ever felt this way?

Now, after going through times of actually having "the shoe drop," I've discovered something I'd like to share. This is life. We all have seasons of happy, fulfilling, and fun days, and we all have our times of sorrow and distress.

Thankfully, something has changed for me. There came a time in my life when I totally surrendered my heart to Jesus, and I learned that He can be trusted. For me, being His child means encountering a place of rest and peace. He has always been there for me. He's been there through it all. He's never left. In the happy times, He adds His joy and in the difficult times, He gives me His comfort, peace, and encouragement.

So now when things are going well, and that old feeling of dread tries to come upon me, I STOP and remember God's faithfulness and the comfort, guidance, and miracles I've experienced in those trying times. I can then enjoy the happiness that I'm experiencing, knowing if the season should change, my Father and Friend is with me. I'm surrounded by His love.

He will be there for you too if you ask Him to be. He only waits for an invitation. He loves you so much! Know that you can cast your care on Jesus because He cares for YOU!

DIGGING DEEPER

1. When things are going well in life, do you tend to worry about what may be coming around the corner?

2. What are some things that God provides that you can count on even when the "other shoe" does drop?

3. Read Psalms 139:16 & 17. When you read and meditate on these verses, what feelings and thoughts surface about the seasons we experience in life?

PRAYER

Father God, thank you for your faithful involvement in my life. Help me to feel your presence in the seasons of sorrow and distress and help me to also remember your faithfulness in the seasons of joy and happiness. Remind me that I can trust your love and tender care for me in every season of my life.

AMEN

Build That Wall

By Ray Painter

One warm spring day, I walked outside our home to see what condition the lawn was in, if there were weeds, and what needed to be done. I turned and looked over to the front door of my house. My son Aaron's bedroom and the living room were in the front part of the house. Aaron was about eight years old, and he and my sons, David and Jon, would play on the hill that sloped down away from our home. They had been playing on this hill for a long time.

As I stood there looking at everything, suddenly, in my mind's eye, I saw a vision of a car hitting that hill and flying right up into the house! We lived one house off Auburn Street in Rockford, and nothing like that had ever happened.

I believed it to be a divine revelation.

God's trying to tell me something. I've got to build a wall!

I took my sons with me, and we went to find the materials we needed. At that time, they were tearing out a lot of old railroad tracks. People would go scrounge them up and sell them. There were railroad ties for sale everywhere, so I found a guy who had some. They were not in very good condition, but I decided to go ahead and buy them. I dug a footing and got the property line struck, and put it just inside the line.

Much to my surprise, only two or three months later at about 10:00 at night, a car came flying through the air and hit that wall! Boom! He had flown completely across my neighbor's lawn, never touching the ground and hit that wall! He had been running from the police and must have been going 50 to 60 miles per hour.

He was at the corner of Auburn and North Main Street, spinning his car around in circles in the middle of the intersection, just squealing his tires. A police officer was sitting at the intersection waiting for the light to change when this occurred. He threw on his lights and siren. It startled the guy and he took off flying down our street. He was drunk, and high, and totally messed up. The accident didn't hurt him at all. We tried to call an ambulance, but he refused the ambulance. He refused any medical help.

This incident taught me to pay attention when God shows me something. I could have easily dismissed it and said it didn't make sense. It takes time and money to build a wall when it seems unnecessary. There was no reason to believe that anything like that would happen. I only knew that the vision was from the Lord, and it was!

The local television station came out to report on what happened and interviewed me. This is what I told them and what I want to share with you.

"That night, God spared my family from a disaster by telling me ahead of time to build that wall. If the wall had not been there, the car would have gone straight through to my youngest son's bedroom where he would have been sleeping. I don't know if he would have been injured or killed. All I know is I'm so thankful that God gave me that vision."

So, the title of my story is, "Build That Wall." And that's what God told me to do—build a wall.

DIGGING DEEPER

There are many examples in the Bible where God told people to do something that didn't seem to make sense.

Can you think of any of these stories?

Why do you think God sometimes operates this way?

1. God wants to speak to us to give us counsel, comfort, knowledge, wisdom, warning, and direction. Read the Bible verses below, then write down a way that God communicates with us:

- Psalms 119:105

- Proverbs 19:20

- John 10:27

- John 14:21

- John 14:26

- Acts 2:17

- 2 Timothy 3:16-17

2. What are some things we can do to help us hear from God?

3. Can anything keep us from hearing God?

PRAYER

Heavenly Father, thank you for the gift of salvation through Jesus Christ that opens the door for relationship and communication with you, my Creator! Wow! It's a wonderful thing to know that you want to speak to me! But Lord, there are so many distractions in this world, so help me in my pursuit to know you more every day for I know that there is life and peace in knowing you. I am excited to hear from you in any way that you want to speak to me. Give me ears to hear and eyes to see what you are saying.

AMEN

Daisies

Ray had a Gideon meeting early one Saturday morning. I got up with him, put some laundry in the washer, and decided to have a quiet time with the Lord. As I grabbed my coffee, I realized my Bible was upstairs. So, I decided to take one of my older Bibles that I hadn't read for a while off the bookshelf. I turned to the back where I had written some notes and dates of significant times when I had prayed and God had shown up.

More than once, when I was going through an especially difficult time, God used daisies to touch my heart and encourage me. I love the beauty and simplicity of daisies. They seem like friendly flowers, and they cheer my heart.

The first time this occurred, I was hurting deeply and I said a silent, little prayer to God about how I would love some daisies. The next day I received a beautiful bouquet of daisies! As I read these reminders of His great love in my

Bible, I was overwhelmed with thankfulness and told God how much I love Him. What a journey this has been!

After Ray had finished his meeting, he stopped by the store on his way home to pick up a couple of things we needed. As he walked by the flowers, he saw a bouquet of colorful daisies and brought them home for me, not knowing anything about my morning.

When Ray walked through the door and I saw the daisies, I hugged him and cried happy tears. I'm so thankful for my husband and I'm also incredibly thankful that through all the good and the bad times, God has been there for me. We were not going through a difficult time. I guess God just wanted to say, "I love you too."

So why am I telling you this? Do I just want to let you know that God loves me?

No! No! No! I want you to know how much He loves YOU! Maybe you've never asked God for daisies. Maybe daisies are not your thing at all. God knows that, and He knows what you need at this very moment. He longs to have a relationship with you so much that He died for you. (John 3:16) He loves us individually and personally.

Maybe you have been trying to do life on your own. I've tried that route, and it's not good. Jesus came to rescue us! It's not about religion, it's about a personal relationship.

He's for real! Trust me, although it's not always easy (no relationship is), it's the best way to live! There are times you may feel alone, but He will always be there if you invite Him. If you've never asked Jesus to be your personal Lord and Savior, he's waiting for you! If you invite Him into your life, you will not be disappointed. He has good plans that He wants to share with you. (Jeremiah 29:11) He loves YOU! It's your choice!

If you want to know more, turn to page 268 at the back of this book.

DIGGING DEEPER

1. Psalm 34:8 is an invitation to experience the goodness of God. What are some things in your life you might sometimes take for granted that are evidence of the goodness of God?

2. Have you ever had a situation where you prayed for something specific like Nancy did with the daisies?

3. Do you feel closer to God's love and kindness during the challenging times of life or when life feels easy?

PRAYER

Father God, I invite you into this day and whatever it may hold. I thank you Lord, that I am held by you, loved by you, and even celebrated by you! Thank you for knowing my needs before I even tell them to you. Thank you for your generous love and for the ways that you show it to me personally. Help me to grow daily in my relationship with you so that I can experience your love to greater levels and be an extension of that love to others in a hurting world.

AMEN

Deep Cleaning

✻

My husband Ray and I decided to put a house we owned up for sale. The renters who had been living there left us with quite a mess. It was a beautiful home that I had lived in before we got married. After we married, we decided to rent it out, but we had become weary of renting and wanted to be free from it. I loved the home, and it hurt my heart to see it so neglected and abused by the last tenant.

After working there for almost two months, it started to come back alive. My hope was that the people who would buy it would make it a real home again, not just a place to live.

Meanwhile, because we were working so much out of town in Winnebago, our own home had started to show signs of neglect. After driving to Illinois and working all day and then driving home, my energy had been depleted by the end of the day. Our home had been getting what my mom called, "a lick and a promise."

One night I came home to a surprise. When I walked in, everything shined and the fragrance of red apples from my wax warmer filled our home! My daughter-in-law Ariel had asked if she could do laundry at our home as she wasn't able to get to the bank to get enough quarters for her laundry. (At the time there was a shortage of coins.)

While she was there, my home got what she called a "deep cleaning", and it showed! I was so thankful!

That night as I was enjoying the freshness and comfort of my home and listening to the rain, I started talking with God about the day. I thought about Ariel's words...deep cleaning.

I wondered, *in my busyness and tiredness, had my soul gotten a little dusty too?* Were there some cobwebs entangling my mind? Had I neglected some deep cleaning? Maybe I still looked okay on the surface, but I started thinking it was time to stop and get to the places that no one sees.

When Jesus looks into my heart, what does He see? When He returns for His Bride, will my "house" be clean and in order? So, my prayer that night was, "Wash over me Lord, that I might be truly cleansed and shine for you.

DIGGING DEEPER

1. As a follower of Jesus, what are some disciplines that are important to your faith but can be easy to let go of amongst the busyness and distractions of life?

2. What are some signs of neglect when it comes to your spiritual life that indicate it may be time to do some deep cleaning?

3. Walking in a deep relationship with God sometimes takes some deep cleaning. Describe what a deep relationship with God means to you. Now describe what a deep cleaning might mean to you.

PRAYER

Lord, show me those areas of my walk with you that I may have neglected. My relationship with you is the most important thing, but I know sometimes I don't treat it that way and I'm sorry. I don't want just a surface relationship; I want to be in a close relationship with you. So, whenever a "deep cleaning" is needed, help me be quick to get rid of those things in life that aren't important but may take up a lot of my time and attention. Clear the cobwebs from my dusty soul today, Lord! Make me fresh and new and clean! In Jesus' name.

AMEN

Dirt Perspectives

DIRT AT SEEN THROUGH THE EYES OF A MOTHER:

It's the enemy.

Sweep it up.

Wash it away.

Get it off of my

children and out of the house!

DIRT AT SEEN THROUGH THE EYES OF A CHILD:

Just add some water and it becomes instant fun!

It makes
delightful
mud pies
and feels
wonderous
squished
between my
fingers and
toes. It's

known to cause giggles!

DIRT AT SEEN THROUGH THE EYES OF A GARDNER:

A place to

create beauty

and feel renewed.

A place to grow

fresh,

healthy,

food.

DIRT AT SEEN THROUGH THE EYES OF A GOSSIP:

A juicy tidbit to be whispered in the ear of anyone willing to listen (Proverbs 16:27 & 28)

DIRT AS SEEN THROUGH THE EYES OF A FARMER:

Rich dark soil to fertilize and till to make my living—my sustenance.

DIRT AT SEEN THROUGH THE EYES OF GOD:

Someone to love.

"And the Lord God formed man of the dust of the ground and breathed into his nostrils the breath of life; and man became a living being." (Genesis 2:7 NKJV)

So, if there are times you feel like dirt, remember God loves you and sent His son Jesus to die for you! (John 3:16)

And if you ask Him, He will breathe life into you and any situation you may be facing.

DIGGING DEEPER

Perspective is so important! I learned this lesson several years ago when I was driving home from a very long afternoon of running errands. The sun had set, and I was tired, but I was finally headed home! That's when my husband called and asked me to make one more stop to pick something up for him. I had already passed the store and would have to backtrack. I told him I would do it, but I was irritated, and I let him know it. (I'm embarrassed to admit how much I let him know it).

As I was driving home, the Lord spoke gently, yet very clearly to me. He said that I had the wrong perspective. I was looking at my husband's request as an inconvenience and an irritation when I should be viewing it as an opportunity—an opportunity to show him love! Love that is patient and kind, not irritable (real love as described in I Corinthians 13). When life is easy and everything is peachy, it's super easy to show love. But when we're tired, hungry, angry, (or even just hangry!) we can be anything but loving to those whom we love deeply!

Perspective can change everything! Here's a little experiment you can try the next time you encounter a challenging situation. Think about the prompts below and see if the answers may change your perspective.

- Is there an opportunity in this situation to learn something?

- Is there an opportunity here to show someone kindness or love?

- How can I get my focus off myself and onto another?

- What in this situation do I have control over?

- Is there anything in this situation I have NO control over?

- Is there an opportunity to bless someone in an unexpected way?

- Why am I REALLY feeling irritated? Angry? Afraid? Offended?

- How can this situation teach me to be firmly rooted in trusting God and God alone?

PRAYER

Lord, thank you for giving me the power of choice, even in my thoughts and how I look at things! Help me in every circumstance to choose life and to see things from your perspective, as much as possible, as I walk in your ways. Help me never to refuse to listen to you as you lead me. So today I commit myself firmly to you. Remind me often that your way is the key to genuine and exuberant life! (Deuteronomy 30:15-20) AMEN

Do All Dogs Go to Heaven?

The sound of barking dogs greeted us as we walked through the door of the County Animal Services building. Excitement grew as we signed our names in the log book and entered the room where the dogs were lodged. This was the day we hoped to find a new puppy for our home! As we walked around, it seemed every dog was vying for our attention. Some looked a little intimidating as they barked at us, others pleading. It would be hard to pick just one.

I think Shadow was the third dog we requested to spend time with in the small room that was set aside for getting acquainted with the dogs. When they brought her

121

to us, we noticed she was sweet and timid. Even though it was to be my daughter Mary's decision, our family was in total agreement. She was the one. She was all black with a little bit of white on her chest and feet. Someone had found her on the street and brought her to the animal shelter. She was unsure of herself, but there was a gentle, ladylike beauty about her.

We brought her home and decided on the name "Shadow". It turned out to be appropriate, as she followed us everywhere. We didn't know what breed she was or exactly when she was born, only that she was less than a year old. But now she was ours.

Because she adjusted so easily to our home with very little training, I wondered if someone had started to train her before she was abandoned or lost. We noticed she was afraid of men in hats, but she was not aggressive. Eventually, she became more confident and protective, but always sweet. I had a daycare in my home, and I was never concerned that she would hurt a child. It wasn't her nature.

We all loved her, but Mary was her favorite and Shadow slept with her in bed at night. Mary took her to 4-H Dog Obedience class, and she also taught her to jump up into her arms when she would signal her. It was funny to watch because she was almost as big as Mary, but neither of them minded that. Shadow was loved. She became part of our family.

Daughter Mary with Shadow

We had another older dog for a while, Buddy, a Shih Tzu. Buddy couldn't hear or see very well at the end of his life, and Shadow would look out for him. We had a fenced-in yard and when I'd call them in, Shadow would go get Buddy and he'd follow her into the house.

As my kids got older and became teenagers, Shadow and I would go for walks together. When I'd get home from work, she'd be waiting for me at the door when no one else was there.

At night when I would sit down to read or watch television, Shadow would wait until I put a blanket on the couch. That meant she had permission to jump up and lay down beside me. It was a comfort to have her sit with me.

Grandchildren Max and Mika with Shadow

A few years later, when I married and my husband and I went away to Bible college, Shadow lived with Mary some of the time but eventually made her home with my son, Joe, and his family. While living with Joe and his family, Shadow and my granddaughter, Raedyn, became attached, and Shadow slept with and protected her.

Shadow and I were both afraid of mice. One night I heard something in my kitchen cabinets. She and I stood there, neither of us sure of what we should do. Finally, I said, "Shadow, go get it!" She looked up at me like, "Who, me?" Then, I'd never seen this before, but she tiptoed into the kitchen and then tiptoed back and stood by me. She

Shadow
wearing goggles

looked up at me as if to say, "There, I ventured in and made it back." I remember laughing out loud and telling her she was not earning her keep!

But when she lived with Joe and his family, she became "Shadow the Mouse-Hunter." If Joe saw a mouse in his garage, he would call her downstairs to the garage and the hunt was on! Usually, she'd catch it! I still haven't figured that out. Maybe Joe's courage rubbed off on her.

Joe and his family made a decision to move to Madison, Wisconsin, and our granddaughter Raedyn had to leave her friends. Melanie, my daughter-in-law, told me that Shadow became Rae's best friend. They would even play dress-up and Shadow was such a good sport about it. Eventually, Rae started school and made some new friends. Shadow was introduced to them and loved by all.

It was hard to watch as Shadow started going downhill. It seems her last year, Joe was the one she "shadowed". I wonder if Shadow felt that Joe was now her protector in her frail years.

Joe, Mel, and Rae took such good care of her as she slowly declined. I knew the last time we saw her that we were saying goodbye. We estimate that she lived 19 years. She was especially close to us all in different ways and at times when we really needed her.

Raedyn took this selfie of her and Shadow.

About that question—do all dogs go to heaven? I can't find in the Bible a verse that says for sure one way or the other. But there are many places where it talks about the animals that will be there. It's going to be beautiful, unspoiled by any kind of evil, the way God originally intended it to be before man decided to do "his own thing".

The Bible says the wolf will lie down with the lamb, and snakes won't harm children. (Isaiah 11:6-8) The rivers and lakes will be crystal clear and there will be trees abundant with delicious fruits. It's a place where God wipes away all our tears. There will be no more death, sorrow, or pain, and Jesus will be there! These things I know!

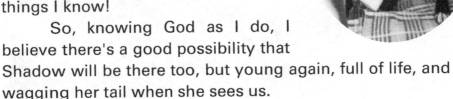

So, knowing God as I do, I believe there's a good possibility that Shadow will be there too, but young again, full of life, and wagging her tail when she sees us.

And if you're not sure that you will be going to heaven yourself and would like to know, please turn to page 268. There is an answer to that question.

DIGGING DEEPER

It's so easy to get caught up in our day-to-day schedules and all that is going on in the world. But it's good to remind ourselves that this world is not our eternal home. I believe God also uses the events that we all experience in life to remind us of that.

Read Revelation 21:1-5.

1. What feelings or emotions do you feel when you think about heaven and what it might be like?

2. What aspect of heaven are you most looking forward to?

3. What part of life on earth will you be happy to leave behind?

PRAYER

Dear Lord, even the most splendid beauty of this world and the greatest joys in my life must be but a glimpse into what heaven will be like. Even in the most wonderful times, there is still that longing and knowing inside that more—and better—lies ahead! When I experience trials and chaos, sadness and grief that are inevitable in this world, draw me closer to you, Jesus, and whisper in my spirit the hope of my eternal home. When that hope is reignited in me, I can't keep it just for myself. I want to point others to your unending hope and immeasurable love! As I put my trust in you, Jesus, day by day, help me to grow more heavenly-minded and see things more often from an eternal perspective.

AMEN

Dull Women Have Immaculate Houses

It was a last-minute decision. I jumped out of bed and hurried to get ready! Hopefully, I could make it in time! Being a person with a rigid routine, it was difficult not to make my bed. My mother had taught me as a young child that this was the way to start your day. It had stuck with me, and even though my daycare business was often chaotic, it felt like there was some order to my life when I climbed into a well-made bed at the end of the day.

My normal week consisted of caring for eight to twelve children ranging from newborn babies to twelve-year-olds, working ten to twelve-hour days. I had a routine and followed it faithfully. I worked five days a week, cleaned the house, and got groceries on Saturday. Sunday, I went to church, relaxed, and spent time with family and friends.

But today I was breaking my own "rule." When my friends asked me to join them on a trip to Six Flags Great America (an amusement park about an hour and a half drive away), I wanted to go. It sounded like fun, but how would I get the house cleaned? How would I get my bookkeeping up-to-date? I was responsible to make sure that everything was ready for Monday morning! I reluctantly told my friends no.

But Friday night I talked with my daughter, Denise, who lived next door to me. She said, "Mom, you need to go and have some fun!" I thought about it, and so here I was, early Saturday morning, leaving behind a mess and heading to Great America

As I pulled into the church parking lot, I saw that the bus was still there! My friends were happy to see me, and we talked and laughed on the way to the park. I made a decision, along with some encouragement, to ride every roller coaster in the park. This was way out of my comfort zone! But I was pretty excited about it!

We worked our way through the park, hitting every roller coaster. It was an amazing day with some fear, lots of excitement, good food, and laughter! I almost felt like a kid again. I went home feeling happy and victorious! I had conquered giant roller coasters, overcome some of my fears, and had so much fun doing it!

As I drove into my driveway, I knew that I had filled the day with wonderful memories and would just have to pay the price.

I walked up to my bedroom door and there on my messy bed, propped up by pillows was a small plaque! As I looked at it, I laughed out loud. My daughter, Denise, had "stumbled" on it during the day and bought it for me. She had carefully placed it in the middle of the mess where I would see it. It read, "**_Dull women have immaculate houses!_**"

I carried it to the stairs and sat down. As I pondered it, overwhelming love and joy filled my heart! My daughter had cared enough to buy this for me. She is a treasure to me!

But even more than that, I felt God's love. I know God directed Denise's steps that day, and when she saw it, she knew it was for me. God knew that I often felt guilty if I spent time or money on myself. I don't know why, but I did. I know it was not God that made me feel that way.

That day sitting on the steps, I felt free! I believe God was showing me that as His child, he wanted me to have some fun and enjoy my life! Even though I had much catching up to do, when I laid my head on my crumpled pillow that night, I felt a wonderful peace and joy!

My conclusion—be responsible and work hard, but take time to enjoy the people and the life God has given you!

DIGGING DEEPER

1. When was the last time you experienced the joy of feeling like a kid again? What were you doing?

2. Jesus' first recorded miracle was at a wedding celebration when He turned water into wine for the wedding guests. Do you picture Jesus as someone who not only attended a party but wanted the wedding guests to enjoy their celebration? Why or why not?

3. Read Matthew 11:28-30. Are there any areas of your life where you are weary or carry a heavy burden? Invite Jesus into those areas now and ask Him to give you rest (physical, mental, and emotional rest).

PRAYER

Heavenly Father, thank you for Jesus who takes my weariness and heavy burdens and in return, gives me the real rest that my soul needs. You have an abundant supply of freedom and grace for me. Teach me how to walk in it each day, so that I can find renewal in my soul and be a person who overflows with peace and joy in a world that needs it so desperately. I know that this is not something that I can do in my own strength, and I thank you Lord that I don't have to. Today, I am thankful for all the wonderful blessings you have given me in life, and I choose to enjoy them!

AMEN

From Torment to Freedom

By Denise Monson

From about the time I was 17, I started experiencing something very scary. I didn't know what it was, but it felt evil. I would wake up in the night from a bad dream, feeling paralyzed and not being able to move. It felt like something was in the room.

I knew that my only hope was Jesus. I would try to speak out loud the name of Jesus, but I couldn't speak. My mind was awake, but my body wouldn't move. It was terrifying—my heart would race, and it was always very difficult to fall back asleep.

It was also very depressing because I hadn't heard of anyone experiencing anything like this, and I really thought people would think I was crazy if I talked about it. (This was before Google could answer all our questions!)

This went on for many years. Thankfully, it didn't happen often. When it did, the only thing I knew to do was to get up and pray and ask Jesus to rescue me. When my

135

daughter was born several years later, it was happening more frequently. With the added sleep struggles of having a newborn and trying to function at work and also as a wife and mother, I was feeling desperate and depressed. At a time when I should be enjoying my beautiful baby girl, I was sleep deprived and in survival mode.

One night at church, the pastor was praying for people and calling out the problems they were experiencing—"someone here has been dealing with a pain in their right knee", or "someone here has been having issues in their shoulder" and things like that. ***Then he said, "someone here has had a tormenting spirit visiting them in the night."*** WHOA! It was like a lightning bolt hit my heart; I knew he was speaking directly to me! At that point of desperation, I didn't care what people thought; I went up for prayer. I wanted to be free!

After that night the episodes got fewer and far between until I no longer experienced them. Praise God!!! I still dealt with insomnia though. That was not fun, but compared to what I had been dealing with for so many years, I wasn't going to complain!

A few years later, I went to Ukraine on a mission trip, I was having trouble sleeping every single night. This was such an exciting time for me being on my first mission trip, but it was hard to function with barely any sleep. Nevertheless, I made a decision that I would just trust God to help me through it.

Towards the end of the trip, my mom who was with me on the trip, and a couple of other ladies who were also there, prayed for me in the cafeteria of the orphanage we were visiting. The night before we were to return home, I

still didn't sleep!!! I just laid there for what seemed like an eternity, praying, "God, I don't understand this! Why can't I just SLEEP?!! Nevertheless, I trust you, I trust you, I trust you! Even without sleep, I will be OKAY, and I trust you!"

The night that I arrived home, I hadn't seen my husband and kids for a week, and I just wanted to be with them, but I kept falling asleep! I chalked it up to jet lag and the lack of sleep during the trip, but ever since that point, I have been able to sleep! Almost every night I fall asleep and stay asleep! If you've ever dealt with insomnia, you know what an awesome gift it is to sleep through the night. I don't understand why I went through that for so many years, but I feel like I have learned a few things:

- God does not put these things on us—fear, sickness, anxiety, depression. He doesn't have those things to give us. He is GOOD! He is LOVE! Those things are not from him. He wants us to be free! (John 10:10)
- Satan's tools are lies. In the Bible, he's called the "father of lies." He tells us things like, "No one will understand what I'm dealing with; They'll think I'm crazy if I talk about this; This is my fault, I must have done something to deserve this." Isolation, Lies, Fear, Shame, Intimidation—these are his weapons of choice. Remember, the Bible says, the devil prowls around, "seeking whom he may devour." (I Peter 5:8 ESV)
- When we pray and the answers don't come, we must continue to have faith that God loves us! He wants us to be free, to have joy, to have peace, both now and in eternity. We don't know the whole story but we can know that He IS good, and He IS love. Even when we

don't understand, the best thing we can do is to trust Him.

Whatever you may be struggling with, know that God cares! It may not always feel that way, but the truth is He does. His plans for you are always good (Jeremiah 29:11); He will never leave you or forsake you (Deuteronomy 31:6). There IS an enemy of your soul, he IS evil; there is NO good in Him and he has nothing good planned for us. Eternal separation from God is his ultimate goal. But God is calling each one of us—urging us to choose Him! Choose His way! Know Him! He urges us to have a relationship with Him, and learn how to trust Him.

Do it today! It's really very simple, not always easy, but simple! (Turn to page 268 to read more!) I'm still learning, and I don't have all the answers, but I know one thing—God loves you! Choose Him!

DIGGING DEEPER

In John 10, Jesus calls himself the Good Shepherd and says, "I have come that they may have life, and that they may have it more abundantly."

1. What does abundance mean to you? How do you think God might use the trials of life to move you from "just getting by" to living more abundantly?

2. Think about a past or current struggle in life. Does your perspective (or feelings) about it change if you consider it as an opportunity to grow in your understanding of God and your trust in Him?

3. In a past struggle that you can remember, what specific ways did God show you that He did not leave you alone in the struggle?

PRAYER

Heavenly Father, thank you that no matter what comes my way in life, and no matter the outcome, you can be trusted. So, now, I trust you to show me what I need to know when I need to know it. I trust you to walk by my side, to surround me with your love, and to see me through to the other side of the trials of life. Thank you for continually helping me to grow in my understanding of you. Guide me Father to new levels of freedom, peace, and joy as I rest in your goodness.

AMEN

God's Menu: Biscuits & Gravy

My husband, Ray, and I are involved in jail ministry. One night one of the inmates was sharing with Ray that he had been in and out of jail several times. This time in, he has decided to get serious about his relationship with Jesus.

One morning as he was walking around the gym in the jail praying, he thought, "I would sure love to have some biscuits and gravy," so he decided to ask God for it. Immediately he felt guilty for praying what he felt was a selfish and unimportant prayer. He told God he was sorry and that he knew there were so many other things that he should have been praying about.

He went on walking and then headed for the commissary for breakfast. As he approached the breakfast line, he looked down the line, and to his surprise, they were serving biscuits and gravy! This was not on the planned breakfast list, and he knew it. When it was his turn to be served, he was given an extra-large serving, more than the others around him! As he walked away, he felt in his spirit the Lord say to him, "I love you!" He needed to hear that.

It is so wonderful to know that wherever we are and whatever we are going through, God cares. The God that formed the earth, placed the stars in the sky, and calls them by name* cares for us individually! If we will call out to him, he will answer us.

Whether we live in jail or in a penthouse, He loves us and looks at our hearts, not our addresses. Wherever we are He will find us! There is no prayer too small or too big for him! He loves us more than we can even begin to understand. The Bible says that God not only loves us but that GOD IS LOVE!** Isn't that amazing?

If you've never experienced His love and want to know more, I invite you to turn to page 268 to understand more about His amazing love for you.

DIGGING DEEPER

1. The Bible tells us that God IS Love. Read 1 Corinthians 13 and think about how love is described. Do you think of God as patient and kind? Do you think of God as never giving up on you?

*Psalm 147:4
**I John 4:8

2. Have you ever prayed to ask God for something and then felt guilty for asking?

3. Recount a time, or situation, or area of your life where you felt that God blessed you with an "extra-large serving."

PRAYER

Dear Lord, you have formed the earth, placed the stars in the sky, and you call them by name, and yet, you still want to know me and be known by me! I don't fully understand it, but I am grateful! Help me every day to grow in my relationship with you and my understanding of just how awesome you are!

AMEN

Here Comes the Judge

These statements and questions all have something in common. Maybe you've already guessed it. The people making them are all making judgments based on their own paradigms. Sometimes it's hard not to do. I'm sorry to say that a while ago I found myself making a judgment about someone. Hard to admit, but true.

As I was talking with my husband about the situation, he made a statement that hit home and took me by surprise. It has stuck with me. It was kind of a "wow" moment that opened my eyes. I'm thankful for his insight.

Before I share it with you, let me ask you this—Have you ever been judged? Most or all of us have at one time or another. You know or feel that someone is thinking ill of you. You don't measure up to the standard someone else has set for you. It's not fun! People don't even have to say anything sometimes, as you can feel the atmosphere. You don't feel free to be you.

I know we think of hate as the opposite of love, but I think judgment is in there someplace too. The Bible says that love always believes the best! (I Corinthians 13). Wow! Imagine what it would be like if we all believed the best of others. Of course, sometimes we would be let down. But I think that when we believe and expect that people are going to do right by us, most of the time they do. You may be calling me a "Pollyanna" right now, but don't judge too fast! I just might be right. :)

So, this is what my husband said to me— *"Never judge someone's weakness from your strength."*

Think about that for a minute. We all have natural, God-given strengths. They are gifts from God. We may assume everyone else should operate in the same way we do.

The Bible talks about this in I Corinthians 12:12-27. It relates it to a body; the hand is not supposed to do what the eye does! We have different purposes and different functions.

> Everybody is a genius. But if you judge a fish for its ability to climb a tree, it will live its whole life believing that it is stupid.

Some have the gift of teaching, and others helping; some have the gift of mercy, and others have the gift of giving or another gift. Even though we should all show mercy and giving, for some people it is just a part of who they are, and it flows from them. We need each other! We are to help, encourage, and appreciate each other.

Because we are all different, God speaks to us all in different and unique ways. One of the ways God has done this for me is by giving me a picture in my mind of what He is saying to me.

Years ago, while I was worshiping in church, God gave me a picture of a body and the mouth bent over and bit off the hand! As the hand lay on the ground detached from the body and bleeding, the mouth looked at it and said, "How disgusting!" This is an illustration of what backbiting looks like. It's serious! I don't enjoy being around people who are always talking about others. I'm very sure that when they are not with me, they will be talking about me too.

We are instructed in the Bible to take the plank out of our own eye before we try to take a speck out of our brother's eye! (Luke 6:42) What a great illustration that is! It's a serious thing to set ourselves up as a judge. May God forgive me for the times I have been guilty of judging others and not believing the best. My prayer is that God will help me look at others the way He does, through the eyes of love. I can only do this with His help.

DIGGING DEEPER

1. We all know the saying "Don't judge a book by its cover." Have you ever judged someone based on their appearance, but then found out later that you were completely wrong about them?

2. Have you ever been judged unfairly?

3. Who do you tend to be more judgmental and critical towards, yourself or others?

PRAYER

Father God, I know that Jesus lived a perfect life for me because I was incapable of doing so. He died for my sins and rose again to conquer death and give me freedom. I accept and appreciate all that Jesus did, which includes allowing me to live free from a judgmental and critical spirit towards myself and others.

Make me aware when harsh and critical thoughts come to my mind so that I can be quick to repent. And when someone judges me unfairly, remind me that I am yours and that your love frees me from living up to other people's expectations, allowing me to be who you created me to be. Lord, let the reality of your unending grace and love towards me overwhelm my heart so that I can joyfully extend grace and love to others just as you do for me.

AMEN

Hold My Hand

When I was a teenage girl, I worked for my Grandpa Layng, who owned a photography shop on Broadway in Rockford, Illinois. It was a small store with a sales counter in the front. People would stop in and drop off their film to have it developed. In the back of his store, there was a darkroom with all the equipment needed to develop the pictures.

Photography was intriguing to me, and I hoped that eventually, I would be able to learn all about it. The idea of preserving a moment in time, understanding the effects of lighting, and capturing the emotions and beauty of a special occasion, all were a part of the art of photography I wanted to learn. But my grandpa decided to retire and sell his store. Sadly, I wasn't there long enough to learn all I wanted to know.

I still love taking pictures of family and friends. I sometimes ask my husband to stop the car so I can jump out and snap a picture of some beautiful or unique scenery that I have spotted while we are traveling.

As a sales clerk at my grandpa's store, I would help the customers with their orders. One day an older couple came into the store. I'm not sure how old they were, but I'm guessing they were in their 60's. They were holding hands and they looked at each other with so much love. I don't remember if it was a prayer, but my teenage heart felt, *I hope someday when I'm their age, my life will look like that.*

Life happened and I don't ever remember thinking of that moment again. Things did not turn out how I had hoped. Dreams of "happily ever after" were gone and forgotten. At one time, I believed that true love was only for others, but could never be for me.

But God had a different plan! As you may have read in our story, Ray came into my life, and shortly after that, we were married. Three months later we left to go to Bible school in Oklahoma. We were walking into one of our classes and Ray reached over and took my hand. He loves to hold my hand, and this wasn't anything unusual. But this day, all of a sudden, the memory of that couple flashed back into my mind. I started to laugh as I realized we were now that old couple holding hands and so much in love.

I am thankful that I yielded to God and decided to trust Him with all of my future! I know that I could have chosen to be in charge of my life, and our story would have been so much different.

Even though life can be tough at times, I always want to remember that God has a good plan, and I can trust Him! (Jeremiah 29:11) Surrendering to His plan was difficult and scary for me at the time, but what an awesome adventure it has been!

I would encourage you to allow God to have His way in your life. I promise you; it won't be boring! Hang on to God's hand, relax, and enjoy the ride! There will be ups and downs, but He will never let you down!

DIGGING DEEPER

1. Surrendering to God's plan is a step in our walk with Jesus that most of us have difficulty with. What are some of the fears you may have when it comes to trusting Jesus to be your Savior AND your Lord?

2. Fully surrendering to God cannot be done without trusting Him. What thoughts, fears, or misconceptions of God do you think could be a barrier to fully trusting Him?

3. Are there areas of your life that you find easy to submit to God's will and His plan, whereas other areas of your life are more difficult to give to Him? What parts of your life are you trying to keep control of and why?

PRAYER

Father God, I want to trust you completely as my Savior and my Lord. Help me when I need more faith. I believe that as you have said in your word, you knew me and chose me long ago. Since you created me, chose me, and know me, then you know what is best for me. You know what will ultimately fulfill me in life and help me to grow to be more like you. You know my history, my strengths, my weaknesses, my fears, and my dreams and desires— even those I may have forgotten! Your word says that I am your masterpiece! As my Creator, you created me anew in Jesus so that I can do the good things that you planned for me long ago. Help me to trust you and believe that you have a good plan for me.

AMEN

I Do It! I Do It!

My youngest daughter, Mary, is a wonderful combination of fun, sweetness, and joy with a dash of spunk to make life interesting. Her name means "fragrance from God", and she truly brings sweetness and beauty to those around her.

When she was a toddler and finding her independence, I would often say to her, "Mary, who's in charge?" She would look at me with hesitation, and say, "You are, mommy." I'm not sure if I was reminding her or myself of who was in control.

Early one morning during this time, she came walking into the kitchen. I was at my sink doing dishes, making breakfast, or some kind of "mom chore." But whatever I was doing, I remember that moment like it was a picture forever imprinted on my mind. I turned as I heard her come into the room. There stood my partially clothed little girl with tousled blonde hair, carrying her slacks in her hand. As I watched her start to put them on, I could see it was not going to go well, so I asked her, "Can I help you, sweetie?"

"No, I do it!" She then attempted to put both legs in one pant leg.

"Mary, let me help you," I pleaded.

"I do it! I do it!" She was determined.

With both of her legs partially in one pant leg, she tried to stand and walk. She toppled to the floor. Thankfully, it wasn't very far down, and the only thing that hurt was her pride. She decided to allow me to show her where her legs should go in the pant legs. I had a chuckle inside of me but was careful not to let it out.

Something happened to me at that moment as I watched her. The Lord often gives me "pictures" or uses illustrations to teach me or show me things. I was like my little girl. There were times God wanted to help me, but in my own way, I said, "I do it! I do it!" I wanted to be independent when I needed to be dependent on Him. He showed me that He always is there to help and instruct me if I would only ask Him. I still smile when I remember that moment.

Over the years, I've learned to be quicker to ask for His help in big and little things in my life. Life goes so much better when I do this! He's so much wiser and smarter than me! When I get to heaven and see Jesus, I don't want to be singing the song, *I Did It My Way.* I want to look into His face and say, "Jesus, I did it your way, and it was the best. Thank you for being there, for helping me, and for loving me."

Mary and me in Florida

DIGGING DEEPER

1. Do you consider it a strength or a weakness to be totally dependent on God? Why?

2. Why do you think God longs for us to totally depend on Him?

3. Are there situations in your past where you depended on someone or something and were let down? Do you find it more difficult to rely on God in those areas of your life?

PRAYER

Father God, thank you for the blessing of a relationship with you! Sometimes when I really think about it, I am blown away that the Creator of the universe wants to be involved in my life—not just in the big things, but also in the details!

Your Word says that apart from you, I can do nothing. So, Lord, help me to always stay connected to you. I never want to become so self-reliant and self-sufficient that I forget that you are the source of all that I could ever need or desire. I rely on your wisdom and loving care to guide me and guard me throughout my life's journey. I'm not in charge, you are!

AMEN

I Missed It

I didn't expect to miss it. I had prepared myself, studied, thought about what would be best, and I had prayed. Unlike the game of baseball, which gives you three strikes until you're out, sometimes in life, an opportunity comes just once.

This night was my night "up to bat". I jumped in our SUV with all my gear and headed to the county jail. Just as a batter gets somewhat nervous as he steps up to bat, I usually am a little apprehensive on my nights at the jail. I know there's more at stake than winning a game. This is no game!

I arrived a little early, pulled into the parking spot, grabbed my lanyard from my bag, and placed it around my neck. The lanyard held the badge with my picture I.D. that allowed me access into and out of the jail. I walked through the double doors, greeted the guard at the desk, and headed to the chaplain's office.

After everyone had arrived, we gathered together and prayed. There were six of us and we each had an assignment, a different place to go and meet with the inmates. But we all came with the same purpose, to tell these men and women that God loves them and that there is hope for their future.

Soon the guard came and escorted us into the jail. We left the carpeted area and walked through the first set of locked doors onto the cement floors of the halls. As we walked by the first guard station, there was a large glass window where we could see a group of male inmates watching television.

One of the men in our group stayed in that area and the rest of us continued on through more locked doors. Two other men went to a larger group of around twenty men. My husband, Ray, ministers with this group.

There were six locked doors to go through before finally arriving at my destination. This used to be pretty intimidating to me. I can only imagine what it must be like to not be able to leave. The women in my group are in jail waiting to hear their sentences; some will go to prison and others will eventually be released from jail. They are all going through serious battles. We meet in a small room not far from one of the guard stations.

I plugged in the CD player I had picked up from the chaplain's office and put on some worship music I had brought from home. I waited for them to arrive from their cells. The guard told me they were dispersing medications to the women and would be in shortly.

It wasn't long before five women walked into the room; two I had never seen before. One of the girls was probably in her twenties, about the same age as my youngest daughter, Mary. She looked so downcast. When I saw her, my heart went out to her. It was hard for her to even look up, but she had come voluntarily so I knew she was looking for help. After the Bible study, I hoped I could talk with her about her relationship with Jesus. I wanted her to know how much He loved her.

Our lesson was on forgiveness, forgiving others, and forgiving ourselves. Our time went by way too fast with much discussion. Before I knew it, the guard appeared at our door. She informed me that one of the men who was teaching another group was ready to leave. I could go out with them now or stay. If I decided to stay, it might be a while before an officer would be able to take me out. We hadn't prayed together yet, so I told her if they wanted to go ahead, I would just wait for the next officer to take me out.

She left and we started praying. When I looked up, the other teacher and the guard were waiting for me!

Oh, my goodness I need to get going!

I decided I needed to close, but before I could, one of the inmates asked the young girl I was concerned about, "Ashley, have you accepted Jesus as your savior?"

161

Ashley quietly replied, "Yes, I have, but I need to rededicate my life."

We all joined hands and prayed out loud a prayer of re-commitment. When I looked up, two of the girls were weeping, but their whole countenance had changed, and they were smiling through the tears. We all hugged, and it felt joyful in our little room.

Ashley left the next week. I never saw her again.

As I drove home that night, I realized that because I became anxious about the guard waiting for me, I missed it! If the Christian inmate had not spoken up, the whole outcome of the night would have been different. Ashley would have left the group without the opportunity to surrender her life and her cares to Jesus.

The Bible says to be "anxious for nothing." I've always thought that it just meant not to worry. I discovered it's more than that!

When we get anxious, we can't hear the Holy Spirit clearly because our mind is occupied with care and concern about what is going on around us. It's so important that we stay in the peace of God and listen to Him. I'm glad there was someone else on the "same team" as me who listened and asked the important question because I MISSED IT!

DIGGING DEEPER

1. Have you ever been nudged by God to do or say something, but thoughts of worry or fear got in the way?

2. Just as Nancy's purpose in being at the jail that night was an important one, we each have an important purpose in life. Sometimes though, the cares and worries of our day-to-day life can crowd out those things making it hard to remember what is important. Read the verse below and then list those good things that you believe God has planned for you to do.

   "For we are His workmanship, created in Christ Jesus, for good works, which God prepared beforehand that we should walk in them." (Ephesians 2:10 NKJV)

   a.

   b.

   c.

3. "Be anxious for nothing, but in everything by prayer and supplication, with thanksgiving, let your requests be made known to God; and the peace of God, which surpasses all understanding, will guard your hearts and minds through Christ Jesus." (Philippians 4: 6-7 NKJV)

Based on this verse, what action can you take to experience God's peace when your heart feels anxious, and your mind is bombarded with thoughts of worry?

a.

b.

c.

4. How can we be intentional about living "in Christ Jesus?"

a.

b.

c.

PRAYER:

Dear Lord, help me to stay in peace no matter what is going on, and teach me to listen to the Holy Spirit instead of my anxious thoughts. I don't want to miss out on what you are saying to me! Father, remind me to turn my attention to you whenever my heart feels anxious or when fear tries to influence me. I'm so grateful that you have shown me the way to a peace that can overcome chaos, worry, and fear so that I can live a life of purpose in Christ and do those good things that you have planned for me to do!

AMEN

In the Middle of the Mess

❋

During the summer of 2018, our life was totally disrupted. As we slept peacefully one night, Ray awoke to the sound of running water. At first, he thought it was the water softener recycling, but it didn't sound quite right. Jumping up, he ran to the utility closet which is right off our kitchen. He opened the door and was met with a surge of water, totally showering him from head to foot. He quickly slammed the door shut and grabbed a wrench so he could shut the water off from the source. He stood there a moment armed with his wrench and then bravely threw open the utility door. With his eyes partially closed as the water battered his face, he wrestled with the pipe and managed to stop the flow.

Somehow, I slept peacefully through it all just a few steps away from all the commotion! He never yelled or called out for help, but quietly cleaned up the mess and went back to bed. In the morning, I asked him, "Why didn't you yell for me? I could have helped you!" He just said, "I had it covered." That really amazed me. I would have been shouting, "Help! Somebody, help me!"

Even though Ray had mopped it all up, the floor had been soaked and the laminate had buckled from the water. As we looked over the damage and talked about what to do, Ray said, "I think we should call the insurance company. After all, that's why we carry insurance." So, we did.

To our amazement, they got right on it. They sent a company out to clean up the water residue and dry everything up. They brought in huge fans and pulled up all the wood that was soaked to prevent mildew. There was more damage than we thought.

The next day the adjuster came to see us. He was very nice and sat at the kitchen table as he asked questions to try and figure everything out. He told us we needed to get estimates on getting the work done and the cost of the flooring and asked if we needed a check to get started. Ray said, "Not yet. We will get the estimates and get back to you soon." As they talked, I was thinking, *Whoa! He offered us a check!* But I said nothing.

Because we have a crawl space, our water heater, the water softener, and the washer and dryer are all on the first floor and had to be removed. Taking out the water heater would leave us totally without water. The adjuster told us when it came time to have this done, we should go to a hotel. The insurance company would pay for it, and they even made sure we would stay at a hotel where we could bring our dog, Tuxie. We were impressed!

Our home was totally torn up during this time. Everything had to be moved out to put down the new flooring. Thankfully, we have a screened-in porch, but we had to pack and carry everything out of the first floor of our home to install the new flooring. It was a mess!

But then something kind of amazing happened. As we talked, we considered the idea of remodeling our kitchen to make it more functional, and we remembered something. Months earlier, a prophet had come to our church. He had prophesied to both Ray and me, and one of the things he told us was that we had considered doing some renovations to our home, but weren't sure if we should do it, which was true.

He said we would be in our home for a while and to go ahead and do it! Even though we had talked about how nice it would be, we weren't planning on doing any big projects, as it would be expensive and time-consuming. So, we dismissed it and went on with life.

But as we talked about what we should do now that everything was torn up, we remembered his words and decided to follow his advice and go for it. It was not an easy task, as we did a lot of the work ourselves. At times, we were very worn out, and yet through it all, we felt God guiding and directing us.

We felt His help in so many ways. Our son, Richie, helped with moving and installing the water heater. Our great nephew, Josh, went out of his way to help us get the flooring done. It seemed friends and family came at just the right time when we needed them. After it was all done, we were astonished at how it all came together.

One morning as I was standing in our home looking around, I began thanking God for our new kitchen. I then asked Him, *Why would you do this for us, Lord?*

Then the thought came to me, *Now that it looks so nice, maybe He is going to ask you to sell it and go on a mission field.*

As soon as I had the thought, I heard in my spirit, *Can't I just bless you without you thinking I have an ulterior motive? Don't you bless your kids just because you love them?*

I felt gently rebuked and immediately said, "I'm sorry, Lord."

I needed to reconsider my view of the Father and His love. The truth is God is a good Father and He loves to bless His children—no strings attached!

If you find yourself in the middle of a mess, please know that it's not the end of the story. It's just a chapter. Let faith and hope arise. There are brighter days ahead! Jesus really loves you and has good plans for your life! You can trust Him!

May you see the Father for who He truly is, a God of love!

DIGGING DEEPER

1. Read Romans 8:28. When you read and meditate on this scripture, what does this tell you about the nature of God?

2. Think back to a time in your life when everything was a mess. Can you think of something good that may have resulted from it?

3. Read Jeremiah 29:11. God says that His intentions towards us are good. What types of good things can come from a mess? Add something to this list:

- Labor pains bring forth the blessing of new life.

- Renovation and construction are a tearing down of the old to make way for the new and the better.

- _____

  _____

  _____

PRAYER

Father God, help me to remember that YOU are the one who makes a way in the wilderness and streams in the desert. I give my mess to you and trust you to see me through. Thank you for being a good Father who gives me hope and strength for whatever the day may hold.

AMEN

Lost and Found

❋

Often when my husband Ray and I are working on a project, Menards, our local hardware store, becomes like a second home to us. It was one of those times, and we were at the counter in the paint department waiting to get some paint mixed. My purse was in our cart, and I asked Ray, "Would you watch my purse while I run over to the next aisle and look at the discounted paint?"

"Sure," he said. So off I went to check it out. I was there for just a couple of minutes. Well, it might have been a little longer, but not much.

When I got back, I looked around and there was our cart, but Ray was nowhere in sight! I panicked and rushed over to see if my purse was still in the cart. As I approached, I was relieved as I looked into the cart. It was there, sitting in the cart all alone! A stranger was standing next to it. He looked at me and smiled. "Don't worry," he said, "I was watching it for you."

Relieved, I laughed and thanked him. "Now, I just need to find my husband," I said.

In Ray's defense, he is not used to being a keeper of my purse, and he did have a lot on his mind. But I thanked God for looking out for me and my purse that day and for the honest and kind stranger. It still makes me smile thinking of him standing there and waiting for me to get back to my cart.

Even though I usually am very careful about keeping an eye on my purse, there was another time I almost lost it again. My daughter-in-law Ariel, my niece Marianne, and I decided to make a trip to the local Goodwill store. It is one of our favorite places to meet, often followed by a trip across the street for Dunkin Donuts' coffee and occasionally a scrumptious donut.

That particular day, I put my purse in the bottom of the cart and everything I bought on top. It was a good day for "treasure hunting." When we left, I gathered my packages up and was visiting with my niece as we walked to my car. I must have taken my keys out of my purse earlier because I drove us over to the Piggly Wiggly (which has an adjoining parking lot) to buy a few groceries. As I got out of the car, I looked for my purse. I couldn't find it anywhere, and I panicked!

"Marianne, I'm running back to Goodwill! I must have left my purse in the cart!" I left her standing there and ran as fast as I could across the parking lot to Goodwill. While I was running, I prayed, "God please put angels around my purse and don't let anyone steal it! Please keep it safe!"

When I got there, the cart was there, but no purse. I walked up to the checkout counter. My heart was pounding, some of it may have been from running, but mostly from the possibility of my purse being gone forever.

"Do you know if anyone found a purse? I left mine in the cart," I asked the clerk.

"Yes, it's in the manager's office. I will call him for you."

Oh, God, thank you! I prayed quietly.

The manager came out and asked me to describe it and then brought it to me. Everything was intact. I was so relieved and thankful! What could have been, didn't happen. It took me a while to calm down, and I'm even more careful now than ever.

Purses are very important to us because of all the valuables we carry in them. If you're a woman, you totally understand this.

But how much more valuable are our spouses, our children, and grandchildren? Sometimes they will be out of our sight as they go off to school or away to college. Maybe they will even move to Florida like my youngest daughter, Mary!

We can't always be with them or protect them. Maybe you have an aging mother or father and can't always be there for them to ensure they are safe, or a husband or wife who must go away on a business trip without you. There are so many situations that are out of our control and protection!

But one thing we can do is pray and trust God to watch over them and keep them safe. Just as that friendly man stood watch over my purse, we can trust God with our much more valuable treasures—our loved ones.

DIGGING DEEPER

The Bible is full of promises assuring us that we can trust God! It's when we are in stressful situations that the Holy Spirit can bring those promises back to our minds. So, do you have a "go-to" verse that reminds you to trust God in all situations? *(For example: Proverbs 37:5 TLB says "Commit everything you do to the LORD. Trust him to help you do it, and he will."*

If your answer is YES: Here is a challenge for you this week:

1. Commit that verse to memory.

2. Read it in several translations and think about it as you're falling asleep at night! Really meditate on it this week and plant it deep within your heart.

3. When you talk with someone who is facing a challenge or fearful situation, share that verse with them as one that brings you comfort and strength.

If your answer is NO: Here is a challenge for you this week.

1. Ask a mentor, pastor, or friend what their favorite verse is when they need to be reminded that God can be trusted to take care of them. You could also google "Bible verses about trusting God" or even post the question on Facebook.

2. Ask the Holy Spirit to highlight to you the verse that you should focus on this week.

3. Commit that verse to memory and then in the following week, complete #2 and #3 of the first section.

PRAYER

Father God, I trust you not only with my eternal salvation but with ALL the details of my life. My loved ones, my finances, my health—every area of my life I commit to you now. Be Lord of my whole life! I invite you into every problem that I face today or will face in the future. I trust you to guide me, protect me, and give me wisdom just as you have promised. Thank you for your tender loving care.

AMEN

Mika's Story

✦

This is my story, written by my grandma who loves to write as much as I love to draw. I hope it encourages you.

-Mika.

My name is Mika and I'm one of my Grandma Nancy's favorite people in the whole world.

She asked me to share a story about when I was a teenager and going through a rough time. My heart has always been drawn to art—not so much to writing—so my grandma offered to help me with this story.

One morning during this time, I woke up feeling very discouraged. I lay in bed for a while and thought about life and its difficulties. I decided to pray and ask God for help. Then I got up and

headed for the shower. It felt good to wash off the sleepiness, and I began to feel refreshed.

As I reached for my towel to dry off, I stopped and took in what appeared on the towel—a beautiful heart!

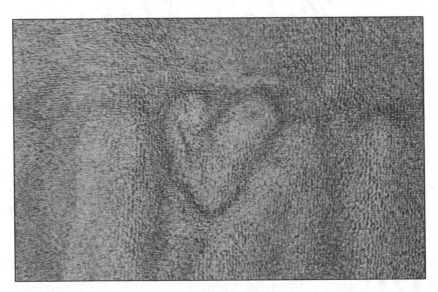

At that moment, I felt God speak to my heart, telling me He loved me. I took a picture of it because I want always to remember that God loves me.

I made it through that time and conquered high school. I'm now in college, majoring in Media Art, and I've discovered college has its obstacles too. I'm thankful to know that God hears me when I pray and that He loves me! He loves you too!

These are some of my drawings that my grandma asked me to share.

DIGGING DEEPER

1. How can you invite God into your difficult days?

2. What helps you keep your eyes on Jesus when you feel discouraged?

3. Read Psalms 116 1-9; Write down 3 ways the Lord responds when we are in need.

PRAYER

Dear Jesus, at times, it seems that I can only see trouble and sorrow in this world. During those times, remind me to call on your name—the One who can save me! You are so kind and so gracious towards me, and when I focus on your love for me, I am restored and renewed!

AMEN

Ouch!

A while ago, I was ironing a shirt, something I seldom do anymore. I'm so thankful we live in a world of permanent press and wrinkle-free clothes: but sadly, not all clothes live up to their label. Maybe it was because I was out of practice, or possibly, because I was in such a hurry, that I burned my finger. It wasn't a big deal, so I just complained a little and went on with my day.

Later I noticed that a small piece of skin was gone and the burn started to hurt. I decided to pay some attention to it and put some aloe vera and a band-aid on it. It healed fairly quickly, but I was left with a hard, callous bump that irritated me. I tried once to peel it off, but that didn't work. (I know, yuck.) So, I waited and slowly it softened and became like the rest of my skin.

So, what's the deal? Why would I even talk about this? Well, have you ever been burned, not physically, but have you ever been hurt by someone, intentionally or unintentionally?

"Well, of course, hasn't everyone?" you might say.

Okay, I agree. You can't live in this world and not get hurt.

Some people might say, "So suck it up, buttercup, and go on." I agree, to a point. I once heard someone say, "When you've been hurt, don't curse it, don't rehearse it, and don't nurse it." It stuck with me. In other words, it's hard to recover when you are thinking and talking about it all the time. When you relive it in your mind, it's like breaking open a wound and not giving it time to heal.

So, we do need to stop dwelling on it and move on. But I also think there is a danger in ignoring it, pretending it never happened. We can become callous and closed up, afraid of getting burned again. We can begin to shut that person, and possibly others, out.

My son, Joe, is a chef. His fingers have become calloused so much that he doesn't have the feeling in them like he used to. He can grab hot pans that we would never think of touching. (Chefs have some superpowers besides making great food!)

So where am I going with this?

Well, here's my thought. There is a remedy. Don't ignore the hurt and become hard, callous, and without feeling. Sometimes we need to talk to the person, *IN LOVE*, and get it resolved. But even before we do that, it's wise to talk to God. He's the only one who really sees it all. He will heal us if we will allow Him to and ask for His help. Sometimes He will even give us a new perspective or insight.

There are times we may not be able to talk to the person who hurt us, but we can and should always pray for them.

"But I don't want to," you might say. Doesn't matter. Do it anyway. It's good for you. It's the only way to truly get healed.

Nelson Mandela said, "Resentment is like drinking poison and then hoping it will kill your enemies." Unforgiveness can actually affect us physically and make us sick. Some burns are small and seemingly insignificant, but it's important to deal with them anyway. It will keep our hearts right.

The Bible teaches about this, and it has proven true in my life. That's my thought for today. I hope it helps someone.

DIGGING DEEPER

1. As you read this, was there a person who came to your mind who hurt you either intentionally or unintentionally?

2. Read Matthew 5:44 and 45. When we love our enemies what does Jesus say it reveals about us?

3. Jesus's instructions are always a roadmap to our freedom and wholeness when we follow them. What things might prevent us from finding freedom after being hurt?

4. Why do you think we sometimes give more attention to the hurt that we experienced than we do to Jesus's instructions for healing?

PRAYER

Lord, show me where my heart may have become hard and calloused towards someone who hurt me. Teach me to take my hurts to you right away instead of rehearsing them and nursing them. You are the great Healer of my heart and know how to set me free from the pain of unforgiveness and bitterness. I don't want to just stuff the pain away; I want to be whole, and I know that you are the remedy. Help me to be obedient and forgive. I can't do it alone, but with your help, I will. Here's my heart Lord, I give it to you to restore and heal and make new today.

AMEN

The Candy Cane Connection

Sometimes we are going along in life and there comes a "suddenly", an interruption in everyday life. Sometimes it's in our own life, but other times we get to watch as a story unfolds in front of us. I'm "the mom" in this story, and thankfully, I got to observe as my son encountered a "divine appointment!"

It was 2011, and our church was having a special family Christmas service in the evening. We decided to go and our son, Richie came with us. When we got there, we looked around for a place to sit. The church was pretty full and excitement filled the air. People were greeting each other and the church looked beautiful and festive. Ray found us a seat and Richie went in first. I followed and Ray sat at the end.

I didn't pay much attention to who was sitting next to Richie, as we were busy talking to some friends we hadn't seen for a while. Then the service began. There was singing, a short funny video with our pastors in it, special Christmas music, and a short message.

Meanwhile, Richie had met the pretty young girl who just happened to be sitting in the seat next to him. She offered him a candy cane; they started talking and romance was in the air! I wasn't aware all this was happening until it was time to leave. I noticed that they were busy talking.

Ray and I started out towards the lobby. Our dear friend, Judy, had noticed the connection that was happening between Richie and this young girl. She told me her name was Ariel and that she attended the Bible study that met at Judy and Warren's home. While attending their Bible study, Ariel had given her heart to the Lord and was growing in him every day. Judy told us she was very sweet. (Good to know!) Since that time, we've discovered it for ourselves. She's a sweetheart!

On the drive home, as we were talking, I mentioned to Richie that Judy knew Ariel. He was very interested! They connected first on Facebook, then on the phone, and then started dating.

A few months earlier, Richie was away at Bible college in Oklahoma, and even though there were many girls there, none of them had the effect that Ariel had on him.

Many people believe that you have to date a lot of people to find the right person. I'm more convinced than ever that this is not true. Sometimes you can get connected with the wrong person that way. I believe Richie knew when he met her that she was the one. They dated about a year before they married, and it's been wonderful to watch as their love story has bloomed and grown. They are a match

188

made in heaven. I know they have obstacles as all couples do, but I know that they pray together. God is blessing them and they are a blessing to others.

We were talking to Richie one day about his second year at Bible school. During that time, it seemed everything fell apart. He was working and attending school. His car broke down and it seemed everything went wrong. We talked with him and he made the decision to come back home. It was a difficult time for him.

As we were remembering this, Richie said, "If all that hadn't happened, I wouldn't have come back and then I would not have met Ariel!"

Sometimes when we are going through a challenging time, it can test our faith. But God has given us promises to stand on when we don't understand. If we keep trusting God, He will work it out for good.

The Bible says, "And we know that all things work together for good to those who love God, to those who are the called according to His purpose." Romans 8:28 What a great promise for those who love God!

DIGGING DEEPER

1. Think about your relationships, past or present. Which ones come to mind as "divine connections" - ones that God may have put together for a specific time or purpose in your life or in theirs?

2. Many people who believe in God mistakenly believe that He created us but is merely a detached observer, not interested in the details of our lives. How does the birth, life, death, and resurrection of Jesus obliterate that belief?

3. In what specific times or circumstances in your life did you feel like Richie - that everything was falling apart? But now, looking back, you can see that God was making a way for something new and better. Think about your life, career, health, relationships, or even your personal or spiritual growth.

PRAYER

God, sometimes life seems so random and chaotic, and nothing seems to be going right. In those times, help me to remember the great love story that is Jesus. You intervened and made a way to save humanity through the great gift of Jesus. How can I believe that a God like that would not care about the details of my life? You are so good, and I have seen your loving kindness and tender mercies countless times in my life. Remind me when things seem to be falling apart and not going according to MY plan that YOU are still in control. You are for me, on my side, in my corner, and You always have a plan for my good and for Your glory. I anchor my life in this truth. I will do what I can do and leave the rest in Your capable and loving hands!

AMEN

The Dance

The other night I was at a dance and didn't know any of the men I was dancing with. It was kind of strange because I knew the man that I was supposed to dance with was there, but I kept missing him. It seemed that I would be dancing with someone when he was free, so we couldn't connect. Another troubling thing was that for some reason, I couldn't hear the music. I could follow my partner, but as hard as I tried, I just couldn't hear the music. It was frustrating. I finally asked the man I was dancing with, "Can you hear the music?"

"Yes, of course!" he replied. Then I woke up. It was all a dream.

This dream bothered me. I love music. Not being able to hear it playing would be awful and missing my partner was disturbing!

Earlier that year I had attended a Women's Conference at our church. Our guest speaker spoke on the meaning of dreams. It was very informative! Did you know that all through the Bible, God used dreams and visions to encourage and give direction to people? He also used dreams to warn them of the dangers ahead. After that conference, I started to pay attention to my dreams and pray about them.

The dream troubled me and a couple of nights after I had the dream I couldn't sleep. I kept wondering about the meaning of it. When we were at the conference, my niece surprised me with a book on dream symbology for my birthday. So, I decided to get out of bed and go check it out.

First, I looked up the word "music". Music represents pleasure, giving praise to God; joyous thanksgiving. I then looked up the word "hear," which symbolically means to be spiritually attuned to revelation; ears to hear releases eyes to see.

As I sat in my living room that night, I knew God was showing me that even though I was in step and following along, I was not in tune with Him. I was busy and not listening as I should have been. I told God I was sorry. It made me sad that I was missing the "music." I know that's where joy comes from!

I thought that was the end of it, but there was more. When we were in church the next Sunday, while worshipping, God showed me the rest. The partner I kept missing was Jesus! He didn't just want to be in the room with me, He wanted us to "dance" together! I started weeping. The idea that I was too busy with other things and was not connecting with Him kind of "wrecked" me. I knew I was missing out!

At a dance, a new partner can tap someone on the shoulder so they can change partners. You let go of the one and connect with the other. I prayed and told Jesus to "tap me on the shoulder" whenever He wanted my attention. I want Him to interrupt my busyness whenever He wants to, so I don't miss what He's trying to say to me. I want to hear His voice and follow His lead.

Since that day, I've noticed a big difference! I have had some amazing "interruptions" in my days! (Read the next story, *Interruptions* for one of them.)

People sometimes view God as a far-off entity who is detached from our personal lives. But He wants to be involved in our everyday life and have a relationship with us. We just need to invite Him in! When we do, we will "hear the music" of life and our hearts will not just follow along but will be filled with joy!

DIGGING DEEPER

Read Job 33:14-15

1. Why do you think God chooses dreams as one of the ways He instructs us, encourages us, or warns us? What are some other ways He can speak to us?

2. The Bible says that Jesus Christ is the same yesterday, today, and forever. This means that God is still speaking to us through dreams and visions! If you asked God for guidance or encouragement in the form of a dream, what would it be about?

3. In this season of your life, would you say that Jesus is merely in the room with you at the dance or is He your partner? Are you dancing with Him exclusively or do you sometimes let other "partners" lead you?

PRAYER

Jesus, I am so glad that you desire to speak to me. I want to hear the music that you are playing, and I also want to be in tune with it! Your word says that you do not abandon those who search for you. (Psalms 9:10) So here I am at the dance, looking for you - don't ever let me go! I believe you are with me during the slow, sad songs and the songs of joy-filled celebration too. Lord when I trip or stumble or forget the moves, be there to guide me with your firm and gentle hand. When the tempo changes and I'm not ready for it, I trust you to lead me through. Let my life be a beautiful dance that is in rhythm with you.

AMEN

Interruptions

※

Stop, Ray! Stop!" I yelled as we started to back out of
the Walmart parking space. I had glanced over at the
car parked next to us and noticed there was a young
woman sitting in it. She was in her early 20's, with multi-
colored hair, piercings, and tattoos, but I didn't see any of
this at that moment. All I saw was that her chin was
quivering and she was about to cry as she talked on the
phone. There was an urgency that reflected in my voice,
and Ray immediately stopped the truck. I reached into the
center compartment and pulled out a small, blue New
Testament Bible.

"Just a minute," I told Ray as I jumped out of the car.
I walked over to her car and said to her, "I'd like to give you
this Bible." She looked at me and put down the phone. and
started to cry.

"Can I give you a hug?" she asked.

My heart filled with compassion, and I said, "Yes, of
course!" She got out of the car, hugged me, and started to
share her story.

She had been physically abused by her father just a couple of days earlier and there were signs of the abuse. She had bruising and lacerations on her face and body, and her leg was wrapped up with a black brace.

We talked for a few minutes, and then I asked her if it would be okay if my husband joined us in the conversation. I told her that he has wisdom that could be helpful.

"Yes, sure," was her reply.

Ray had been in the car praying, and I leaned in the window and asked him to come join us. As soon as he walked over to us, she asked Ray for a hug too. She was hurting, physically and emotionally. As we stood there in the parking lot, she was pouring out her heart and so needed someone to listen. It started raining and was getting chilly, so I asked her if she'd like to go into the Subway inside Walmart and get some coffee.

"You have time for that?" she asked.

"Yes, we do. Let's go," I said.

As we sipped our coffee and talked, we found out that she had a safe place to go in another town and the possibility of a job there. She had also reported the incident to the police and filed charges. The abuse had happened before when her father was drunk, but it had not been as violent as it was this time. She told us that she had gone to her aunt to talk, but her aunt just wanted to tell her about how she had been hurt and how bad her life had been.

"I didn't want to compare who had been hurt the most; I just wanted help," she told us.

We listened and talked some more and then we shared with her that God loves her. She said she knew that

He does. In the past, she had suicidal thoughts, but even though this had been horrific for her, she was not suicidal.

In the back of the little Gideon Bible, there is a page that we call the "GPS" to heaven, "God's Plan of Salvation." There is also another page where you can sign your name if you have decided to receive Jesus as your Savior and date it. She read the Bible verses and told us she wanted to ask Jesus into her life.

I said, "I don't care that we are in Subway; we'd like to pray with you now. Is that okay?"

"I don't care either," she said. "Let's pray."

We prayed together and she accepted Jesus in her heart. She wrote her name in the Bible, dated it, and took it with her. We talked some more before she left and exchanged phone numbers and hugs.

A few days before this happened, God gave me a dream. He showed me in the dream that I was too busy doing things, and I was not listening for Him to talk with me and guide me. I was missing out! I repented and asked Him to interrupt my day any time He wanted.

I believe if I hadn't prayed that prayer, I wouldn't have noticed her at all. Ray and I were really in a hurry to get back to working on a project we were doing. I'm so thankful God interrupted our day! This young girl needed someone at that moment. She thanked us several times for being there.

I know there are people hurting everywhere. Maybe they just need a hug, or someone to listen, or maybe, a friendly smile. I know I have missed it many times, but I hope in the future, I will pay attention to the Holy Spirit's promptings.

It's hard for me to comprehend that as I go about my day, rushing from one task to another, laughing with family, shopping, walking our dog, standing in a line at the grocery store, that all around me there are people who are hurting in different ways. It's not my job to fix it all. Who could ever do that? But I know Jesus! He lives inside me and if I let Him, He can use me to help change or comfort someone! That's pretty amazing!

Most of you who know me, know that I am not an outgoing or forward person. When I look back at that day, I wonder who was that girl jumping out of the car to bring someone a Bible. Was that really me? Really? But I know it was God in me reaching out to let this young, hurting woman know that even though people have used and abused her, He loves her and wants her to come to Him for guidance and healing. Please pray for her.

DIGGING DEEPER

In Luke 19:10 ESV, Jesus states that His mission is to "seek and to save the lost."

1. Why do you think God asks us to be participants with Him in this mission?

2. What resources, gifts, talents, personality strengths, etc. has God given you that can help you to share the

love of God and the good news of the gospel with others?

PRAYER

Lord, make me aware of people you place in my path who desperately need to know you. Enable me to see each person I meet as an image bearer of God whom You love very much. Help me to be an effective, loving ambassador of Christ Jesus. Give me a natural outlet to use the gifts and talents you've given me to impact others with your supernatural love. Teach me to look for the opportunity throughout my day when interruptions may arise. I invite you to interrupt my day anytime you want to!

AMEN

The Miracle of Mary Ashley

My firstborn, Denise, was born when I was 23 years old. We lived in California, away from all of our family. It's incredible to me how awesome she turned out as she was, as some might say, our "practice" baby. There were times I had no idea what I was doing. I wanted to be a great mom, but I'm sure I fell short. And yet, somehow, I ended up with this amazing, beautiful daughter, who over the years has taught me a lot about life.

Our second child was born four years later. His dad was "on cloud nine," as they used to say. He had believed God for a son and was sure he would be a boy. His faith never wavered. I was not as sure as he was about this, but we were all thrilled when our baby boy arrived. We named him "Joseph". He was our little Joey until he grew into manhood and now is known as Joe. He added more joy and excitement to our home.

They were packages of joy with unique gifts and talents. I loved them so much and was thankful for both of them. I felt blessed to be their mom. Even though I was happy with our life, there continued to be a longing in my heart for another child. I tried to ignore it because my husband had said, "That's it. We are done."

This desire continued for many years until one night at our ladies' Bible study, I asked the women to pray for me. I told them that I wanted God to take this desire from me or change my husband's heart. I was 42 at the time. You would think maybe I should have prayed that a little sooner! But that night something changed. A couple of weeks later, as we were visiting with friends who had a baby, my husband looked at me and said, "I think we should have another baby!"

Although I had just prayed for this, I was kind of in shock. I thought God was going to change me, not my husband! Denise was 19 and Joe was 15! Was I sure I wanted a baby at this point in our life? And yet, at the same time, I was very excited. I knew in my heart it was God's plan. He had answered my prayer.

A few months later, I was pregnant. I had a lot of joy, and it seemed it brought joy to all those around me. I loved being pregnant, and I tried hard to do all I could to make sure our baby would be healthy. I tried to eat healthier and made myself drink milk every day, even though I hated it. I started power-walking with some friends in the mornings.

One day after a visit to my doctor, he asked me to come into his office. As I sat there, he described all the possibilities of problems that could occur because of my age. As I walked to the car that day, I remember fear trying to squelch my joy. The statistics were not encouraging at all!

The next Sunday at church, I went to one of the older women in the church and asked her to pray for my baby. It was a turning point for me. It was a time for me to exercise my faith. From that time on, whenever I felt afraid, I would place my hands on my tummy and say, "I thank you, Lord, that my baby is fearfully and wonderfully made according to your plan and purposes." (Psalm 139:13-14) When I prayed this prayer, the fear would go. It would try to come back, but I would just pray, and again, it would have to leave.

Mary Holifield with her namesake.

Another night at church, I felt like we should name our baby "Mary", after our pastor's wife who was a wonderful woman of God. My husband liked the idea and we agreed that was going to be her name.

When I was around eight months pregnant, a group of us from our church went to a Christian seminar in Chicago. Hundreds of people had come to learn more of the principles of how to apply God's Word to everyday life.

During one of the sessions, there was a teaching on how children are a blessing from God. The teacher mentioned that he knew of women who, in their older years, had decided to have another child. He even mentioned the importance of the name of your child. He brought up the name "Mary" and how it could be interpreted to mean "bitter," but he said it could also be

205

interpreted to mean "fragrance from God." I felt like in the midst of that crowd of hundreds of people, God was speaking right to me! My friends were happy too because they knew God had blessed me.

Mary Ashley was born weighing in at 9 pounds! She was strong, healthy, and beautiful. She has been a blessing and a "fragrance from God" to me and to many others.

This is just the beginning of my baby girl's story. She has now grown into a beautiful, sweet woman, and she will write the rest of her story.

Although Mary was planned and very much wanted, I know some children are not planned and some are unwanted. But I believe that God has a great plan for every child, planned or not. Jeremiah 1:5 says "Before I formed you in the womb, I knew you." Psalm 139:13-14 says "For you formed my inward parts; you covered me in my mother's womb. I will praise You, for I am fearfully and wonderfully made." Every baby is wanted and loved by God!

The Lord later blessed me, through adoption, with yet another son, Richie. He also has been a great blessing to our family. You can read more in the next story–*Chosen by Love*.

Mary and me.

DIGGING DEEPER

"Delight yourself also in the Lord, and He shall give you the desires of your heart. Commit your way to the Lord, trust also in Him and He shall bring it to pass." Psalms 37:4-5

1. To you, what does it mean to "delight yourself in the Lord"?"

2. What is a dream, longing, or desire that you have? Maybe it's something you haven't thought of for quite some time or maybe it's been lingering in your heart for many years. Take a moment to talk to God about it. Tell Him everything you feel, knowing that He is a good, safe, and loving God.

3. There are those dreams and goals in life that we know can only be realized with God's intervention. What are some ways that you can invite Him into your plans and "commit everything you do" to Him?

PRAYER

Father God, today, I submit my dreams and desires to your perfect will because you alone know what is best for me. You are the God who sees my hopes and my fears, and you know my heart's deepest longings. You have amazing things planned for me—things that I haven't even thought of or asked for yet! I trust that the dreams and desires that You have put in my heart are safe with you. So, I purpose to put my hope in you and wait patiently for you to work things out for my good and for your glory. Help me not to run ahead of your plan and teach me to keep my eyes on you knowing that my future, my hope, and my joy are found in you, my good and faithful Father.

AMEN

Chosen by Love

***

The first time the idea of adoption entered my mind, I was sitting in our home watching a documentary on television. There had been a war in a country in Europe a few years earlier that had ended. I don't remember anything about where or why this occurred, but when it was all over, there were children left whom no one wanted. They showed pictures of the babies in cribs and there wasn't anyone to hold them or play with them. Only their basic needs for food and shelter were met because there were not enough people to care for them. It broke my heart. I wanted to pick each one of them up and hold and comfort them.

From that moment on, I wanted to adopt. But when I checked into adopting, I found that there wasn't any way for us to do this. Adopting one of these children would cost thousands of dollars. We were a young couple just starting out in our first little cape-cod home and struggling financially at times to make it. So, I put the idea aside, and we went on with our lives.

Two of our children were born while I was in my twenties, Denise and Joe. Then when I was forty-three, Mary was born. After Mary was born, I started taking care of other children so that I would not have to work outside our home. I wanted to be with her as much as possible. Eventually, I became a licensed daycare provider and ran a daycare from my home for ten years. I cared for many children over the years.

This is how I first met Richie. He was in a foster home, and he came to my daycare for a short while. He had been in several foster homes, some of which were pretty poor. His life before foster care had not been good either. His birth mother was involved in drugs and was not able to overcome her addiction. Her children suffered greatly because of this. One of Richie's sisters, who was only a couple of years older became somewhat of the "mother" in the family, as their birth mother would sometimes be absent for days. When she was there, it was not always a good situation either. They even found themselves climbing in the garbage dumps behind Sam's Club for food. In the foster care system, Richie and his siblings were eventually separated, and they were talking about putting him in a group home if they could not find another home for him.

A friend who knew of his situation came to me and asked if we would be foster parents and then eventually, adopt Richie. I was completely surprised by this because I don't remember ever mentioning to her my desire to adopt. I had pretty much given up on the idea, as I was older now and our life was very busy. Whenever I had prayed about adopting, I had pictured a baby or toddler although I don't believe I ever specified that in my prayers. I guess it just never entered my mind to adopt an older child. Richie was nine years old! My daughter, Mary, was ten. This would be a huge change for our family.

My husband and I prayed the night our friend talked with us, and we knew the answer right away. There was no question. Richie would become our son, and so the process began. There were classes to take, questions to answer, and forms to fill out. Was it a hassle? Yes! Did it challenge us? Oh, yes! Was our home disrupted? Oh my! It was never the same. Life was busy already with family and daycare, but this was important. Richie was important!

When Richie came to us, he was on four different medicines, and he had been labeled with a lot of names that are used by social workers and psychologists, but actually really meant he needed love and stability. Who he was had nothing at all to do with the labels that had been given to him. He "acted out" a lot, which I guess means he often disrupted things around him. It's sad to me how our society medicates everything. I'm not against medicine at all. But it is not the answer to every problem.

I remember one day Richie and I were in the waiting room at the doctor's office. He had two small toys in his pocket from McDonald's and took them out to play with them. Another little boy came into the waiting room, and they started playing together. When we went to leave, Richie told the little boy that he could keep one of the toys. At that moment, the Lord opened my eyes and gave me a glimpse into Richie's heart. It was big and kind. After being tossed around and having to leave people and possessions many times, he still wanted to share what he had with others.

After the months of classes and paperwork were complete, the big day finally came! Our family got all dressed up and headed down to the courthouse. After a short wait in the hall, our name was called, and we went into the courtroom.

I remember the judge asking us the question—would we take Richie as our own? As I said, "Yes," to the judge's question, tears filled my eyes. My heart grew and expanded that day, somewhat like the moment the doctor hands you your newborn baby. It was official! Richie was now our son! We went home as a family, but first, we stopped at IHOP for a celebration. The day he was adopted was also my daughter Denise's birthday. It was a wonderful day!

It was not easy blending all our personalities together. There were a lot of adjustments and lots and lots of prayers. It was only a few days after his adoption he got his first spanking in, of all places, a hotel in Disney World. His spanking was followed by hugs and lots of love.

I remember Richie would write his name on things, even the lampshade in his room. It was hard for me to understand this until I realized he was unsure if he was going to stay with us—so much had been taken from him.

Eventually, one by one, he was off all the medicines. We watched Richie grow and change every day into more of whom God intended him to be. I believe some of the medicines actually contributed to covering up the really cool kid that he was.

Some people think adoption is just too hard a process. Others have unrealistic romantic ideas of a beautiful family with no problems. The truth is anytime you bring a child into a family, natural or adopted, there will be changes and challenges. A new baby demands your attention and your sacrifice of sleep and time and energy. But your love gives you the strength to get through the demands of a new baby.

In the same way, an adopted child demands your attention also. Many older adopted children have been through a lot of hurt and instability, things that we can't even imagine. They want to know if this love and family are "for real." They also have become used to looking out for themselves and need to know that they can trust you.

Our family has been blessed by having Richie as a part of it. He is kind, industrious, smart, and fun. He is also one of the most forgiving people that I know. Even though he has had many opportunities to become bitter, he has let go of past hurts. He doesn't dwell on "how bad I had it" or how people have done him wrong. He shares his life story but also tells what God has done for him.

I found a prayer journal in which I had written a prayer for my future adopted child. It was dated shortly after Richie was born. I believe God never forgot my prayer, and God had a plan to bring Richie out of that mess to us.

Even though Richie and his natural brother and sisters were separated, it has been awesome to watch how God has brought them back together and helped them. They have become amazing young adults.

Whitney, Danny, Richie and Britney

Richie is now a grown young man. He married a sweetheart of a girl. They make an awesome team and they both love God and want His plan for their life. I'm so thankful that God blessed us with Richie, and now his beautiful wife, Ariel, is part of our family too. I know God has some wonderful blessings planned for them, and I believe they are and will be a blessing to others.

DIGGING DEEPER

Read Galatians 4:4-7

1. When we receive Jesus as our Lord and Savior, we become a child of God. Why do you think the word "adoption" is specifically used to describe this event in verse 5?

2. When a child is adopted, the course of the life he or she would have lived is dramatically impacted. Read verse 7 and then describe in your own words the changes that take place when God chooses to "adopt" us as His very own child.

3. In this passage, adoption is described as the process of going from "slaves" to "sons." Describe some differences that should take place when our identity is changed from a slave to a free person (a son or daughter of God).

4. A passage in Nancy's story talks about Richie writing his name on all his things because he was unsure about the permanence of his place in the family. Are there areas in your relationship with God where you find yourself feeling unsure or shaky about your status and identity as His child?

PRAYER

Abba Father (Papa, Daddy), thank you for choosing me!
You knew me even as I was being formed in my mother's
womb. You have called me worthy to be your child and
made a way for me through Jesus to be adopted as your
very own. Help me to know deep in my being that as Your
child, I am secure and safe, and I belong. Thank you for
never ceasing to be my Father who loves me, provides for
me, comforts, counsels, and corrects me. When I feel
uncertain and have questions, I know that you are there—
not always to provide answers in the way I might like—but
there to strengthen me and reassure me that you are a
good Father who can be trusted. You heal my heart with
your tender compassion and call me by name saying to
me, "You are mine." Today, I rest in your great love.

AMEN

The Speeding Ticket

by Denise Monson

A few years back, I was driving to our local homeless shelter with enough hot pasta in the back of my van to feed fifty women and children. My daughter and I had been volunteering there with my friend Katie.

I must have had a lot on my mind that night because I took a wrong turn and was going to be late! I started to imagine everyone at the shelter waiting on me to eat dinner! At that thought, I panicked and put my foot on the pedal trying to make up some time when out of the corner of my eye, I saw the police car. Sure enough, the lights started to flash. I pulled over and the officer came to my window asking for my license.

I got the speeding ticket that I knew I had coming to me. After the officer gave me the ticket he asked where I was headed. When I told him that I was running late to serve dinner at the homeless shelter, he seemed to feel remorse for giving me the ticket. My reply was, "No, it's not your fault, I was speeding." And at the time, I meant it—I knew I was guilty.

However, after turning over my hard-earned cash to the traffic clerk as she collected my fine, I started to have a drastically different attitude.

As I was driving home from the courthouse, my attitude began to sour as my thoughts progressed. *I didn't deserve that ticket. I'm a good citizen—I just finished a 6-month stint on grand jury duty—that should count for something!*

Then I began comparing myself to other drivers, *I'm a really good, safe driver. There are a lot of crazy drivers out there that should have gotten ticketed but, No! They don't get caught! I'm the one that gets pulled over! And for crying out loud, I was on my way to volunteer!! This is so unfair!*

As the crazy train of my thoughts progressed, the thought came to me— *Well, you could go back down to the courthouse and try to plead your case!*

I imagined myself going back to the clerk at the window where I had just handed over my cash and saying something along the lines of, "You know, I'm wondering if I could get that money back. You see I don't think I deserved that ticket; you just caught me on a bad day! I'm usually a very safe driver and a good citizen too!"

At that point, I had to laugh out loud at the absurdity of my thinking! As I laughed thinking about the reaction I would get, it was like my own thoughts were interrupted by God's voice saying, *"Don't you see, your good deeds are not a valid payment for your fine."*

Even though I was raised in church my whole life, I still struggled with the concept of "just trying to be good enough" and "shouldn't that count for something, God?"

I didn't realize that calling myself "good" when compared to God's holiness, purity and righteousness is like calling myself "tall" when standing next to Mt. Everest.

Somehow, I had imagined God as a big referee ready to call me out when I broke a rule. I was still learning that being a Christian is not adhering to a list of dos and don'ts, hoping that at the end of my life, my "good deeds" will outweigh my sins.

God knew that in our humanity we did not have the means or the capacity to pay the wage for breaking His law. But because he is a good and righteous God, He MUST punish all sin.

Have you ever heard the story of the criminal who went before the judge and said "Judge, I heard you were good, so I'm betting you'll let me off easy!"? The judge says, "No, it is BECAUSE I'm a good judge that I must see that justice is carried out for the crimes you committed."

God said "It is finished" You're free. Jesus paid the fine and bought our freedom!

So, God must punish ALL sin, but because God IS Love and He loves us so incomprehensibly much, He had to make a way for us to be reconciled to Him, to have a relationship with Him again. That way is Jesus Christ who was also pure and holy and righteous but was punished as if He were the one who had committed our sins. He was treated as a criminal, paying for our sins with his life. Even though He never sinned, He stood in our place, took our punishment, and paid our fine. God said, "It is finished" You're free. Jesus paid the fine and bought our freedom!

Acknowledging that we broke the law and cannot "bribe" God with our good deeds to earn our salvation is crucial! It's when we realize that only Jesus can save us that we become free! Putting our hope and trust in Him alone is what frees us from sin, from shame, from guilt, and ultimately from an eternity without God.

This was an area that I needed to understand more deeply. I love that God cared enough about me to show me in a way that I really "got it". Salvation is not something that can be earned but it's a gift that He freely offers to EVERY one of us. THAT is the Good News!

DIGGING DEEPER

Read Ephesians 2:8-9.

1. What thoughts come up as you meditate on these verses? Do you identify with either of the statements below?

   • "I feel relieved—I know that I'm not good enough to save myself."

- "I feel worried—I still feel like I need to try and measure up with God."

2. Do you ever feel "more saved" or "less saved" based on what you do or don't do?

3. As you dig deeper into your heart, are the good things that you do in life a result of the love that you have for God or an attempt to earn the love of God?

PRAYER

Lord Jesus, help me to understand fully and to my core, that you have paid the price for my salvation—in full! You have done all that was needed to make me righteous and in right standing before God. Even when I don't feel spiritual enough or good enough, remind me of the truth that I am a child of God bought by the precious blood of Jesus. Help me to share the good news of the gospel with those you bring across my path so that they can experience the free gift of your salvation.

AMEN

What Not to Wear

One night a while ago, I pulled my husband into watching a television program with me. I hadn't seen it for a while and was excited to watch it again. It's called *What Not to Wear*. I explained to him that it's a series in which friends and family nominate a candidate for a makeover in clothing, hair, and makeup. Most of the time the people who nominate her feel her style is holding her back from the goals she wants to achieve. They surprise her and show footage of videos secretly taken of her wearing inappropriate or out-of-style clothes.

It's so much fun to watch the transformation! But almost always it takes some convincing for the nominees to throw away their old clothing. But this is part of the deal. She must allow the people who are instructing her to throw out whatever clothing they feel she should not be wearing. In exchange, she is flown to New York and is given $5000 to spend on new outfits! Most of the time, it is an emotional experience. Surprisingly, there is an attachment to the old. It is comfortable and somewhat a statement of their identity.

223

As we watched, I noticed as this woman gave up some of her clothes to the trash that I had some similar clothing. This has motivated me to do some updating! (Anyway, I'm getting a little off track.)

As the program continued, the woman cried more than once and almost decided to quit. But the fashion experts encouraged her, and she decided to keep going forward. As we sat back and watched this, we wondered— *My goodness, why wouldn't she want to give up that!* When it was over, the transformation was amazing! Her confidence and demeanor changed before our eyes.

After she returned home, they interviewed her, and she talked about how this change was helping her. Then she said something that caught my attention. "It's hard to go back to your old ways when you've thrown everything out."

I've been thinking about that. I don't believe in change for the sake of change, but many of us stay in the same place even though it's a wrong fit because it's comfortable and we are used to it. It takes effort to change. They say it takes 21-28 days to change a habit. What a struggle that can be during those times. My daughter-in-law, Melanie, decided to quit smoking several years ago. She told us about the arguments she had in her head, but she courageously fought the battle because she wanted to be free and healthy, and now she is! I admire her and her determination!

I understand how sometimes change is difficult. When I asked Jesus to come into my heart and was born again, He gave me a brand-new spirit, but my mind, emotions, and body were NOT new. They were used to thinking the old thoughts and feeling some emotions contrary to what is pleasing to God.

As I began to listen and follow Him, He asked me to surrender some of my old "clothing." They were dirty, torn, and didn't fit me anymore, but in some ways, they were so comfortable. In place of the old, He revealed to me that He has "clothing" that is so much better! I can be clothed in love, righteousness, peace, joy, and much more as I surrender to Him my old ways! It is my choice!

It's been an exciting journey as I throw out some of the old "clothing" for the new, I begin to see transformation.

It is an impossible task without staying in God's Word and listening to the Holy Spirit. He is the one who encourages

> As I throw out some of the old "clothing" for the new, I begin to see transformation.

me and gives me His grace and direction. He also comforts me as I surrender to him the ways and attitudes that are not good, but almost seem to be part of me. I'm sure there are still some things in my "closet" that need to go, but as I see the transformation in my life, I want more! More of God! It's clean and fresh, and new!

DIGGING DEEPER

1. Why do you think we sometimes have a difficult time giving up the "old clothes" for the new ones that Jesus has for us?

2. Some of the old "clothes" that Nancy describes as old thoughts or feelings may seem so comfortable and familiar that they feel like a part of us. What are some familiar thoughts or emotions that God may be urging you to abandon for His new "clothes"?

   • Thoughts About God

   • Thoughts About Yourself

   • Emotions

3. Read and meditate on II Corinthians 5:17 and then, for each of your answers above, write a new or better

thought, emotion, or feeling that God may want to give you in place of the old.

PRAYER

Father God, as your child, help me to trust you enough to hand over my old "clothes" in exchange for the new ones that you have for me! Thank you, Jesus, for purchasing not only my eternal salvation but also a new way of life! Holy Spirit, lead me daily into the truth that frees me to leave behind the old and embrace the new that you have for me!

AMEN

What's Your Perspective?

Years ago, I spoke at a women's retreat. I began by holding up the drawing of an old woman, or a young woman, depending on your view. I asked how many of the ladies saw a young woman and several women raised their hands. Then I asked how many saw an old woman and the rest of the group raised their hands. It was funny to see them look at each other as they tried to figure out how anyone could see the opposite of what they were seeing.

Today, we see so many different views and because of social media, it has become intensified, as many align with one "side" or another. Sad to say, but some don't want to understand another point of view but only want to "win" an argument.

A while ago, I read a historical novel titled, *Candle in the Darkness* by Lynn Austin. The time period and characters are from the Civil War. Families were divided and people who loved each other deeply were separated by a fundamental truth—"All men are created equal and endowed by their Creator with certain unalienable rights."

There was a line from the book that struck me as profound. The heroine of the book is a Southern girl with "Northern views" whose family owned slaves. She asks one of her dear servants, who is like a father to her, how can we change people's minds. He was a Christian man and told her that you can't; there has to be a change of heart before the mind will change.

I believe at the core of most arguments is pride. Only humble people will actually listen to another person's point of view without an agenda to prove them wrong. Pride is hurtful to both the person who exhibits it and to those around him or her. The Bible says, "God resists the proud, but gives grace to the humble." James 4:6

Sometimes how people present themselves is so loud and offensive, it's almost impossible to listen to what they are saying—It ends up pushing others away. Social media seems to intensify this. I think if we could picture ourselves sitting down with a cup of coffee and discussing our different views, it would help soften our words. Maybe it would diffuse some of the animosity that flies across the internet. Nothing good comes from spewing out offensive, judgmental, angry words.

So, what's my point? Well, the Bible says "to speak the truth in love." Even if we do have truth to present, when we try to "shove it down others' throats," they will not listen to us. If we use vulgar and angry language or come across as condescending, most people will just turn away.

Dr. Martin Luther King is still highly respected because of how he presented the truth he wanted to convey. One of his famous quotes is, "Love is the only force capable of transforming an enemy into a friend. Darkness cannot drive out darkness; only light can do that. Hate cannot drive out hate; only love can do that."

I have some strong views that I feel passionate about, but I pray that I will not just say whatever I feel like at the expense and hurt of others. Sometimes our views will offend people, but if we present them in love and at the right time, they are more likely to be heard.

As the women at our retreat learned to take another look at the drawing, they were better able to see it from another's perspective. There were a lot of "Oh wow!" moments and some laughter.

Will we ever be able to totally agree? Probably not. But that's okay. If we are motivated by love and really listen, we may help each other and possibly learn something new.

Jesus said, "A new commandment I give to you, that you love one another; as I have loved you, that you also love one another." John 13:34

DIGGING DEEPER

Read Proverbs 13:10

1. Is there a way to determine when you are speaking from love and when you are speaking from pride, emotion, hurt, or some other source?

2. When in a discussion with someone of another viewpoint, do you lean more towards listening to understand where they are coming from or trying to convince them of your perspective? Why?

3. Remember a time when you had a discussion with a person who had an opposing viewpoint. How did you feel at the end of the discussion? What did you learn from it?

PRAYER

Lord, I want to stand out and be different from the culture I live in today. I believe that one way to do that is to allow others to be heard and to try and understand where they might be coming from. I know I need your help to do that. Give me grace and love for others, especially when we disagree. Help me to remember that every person I encounter is a person that you created and love dearly. Give me pause to hear your instructions on when to speak and when to stay silent. When there is truth to be spoken, help me not speak from pride but from love and gentleness. Remind me often to view things from an eternal perspective, so that my goal is always to point others to You with the life I live and the words I speak.

AMEN

When God Doesn't Answer

Years ago, when my daughter Mary was a baby, I was trying to transition her into being able to go to bed without me rocking her to sleep. As much as I loved rocking her, she was old enough that she needed to be able to lie down and go to sleep on her own sometimes.

I'm pretty sure that the first night I tried it, I caved, and honestly, I think I caved more than one night. I couldn't handle her sobbing for me, but I knew as a parent, I had to help her make this transition. I needed to be strong, but sometimes I felt it was as hard on me as it was on her. I had such wrestling going on inside of me. As a mother, I wanted to hold her and comfort her, and yet, I knew it was time. I would still have many times rocking her to sleep, of course, but I knew the every-night routine had to end.

So, I resolved one night I was going to stay strong. I rocked her awhile and then loved on her and laid her in bed. She cried as I left the room and said goodnight to her. After she had cried for a few minutes, I would go into her room and comfort her. I would tell her it was okay, I was still there, and then I would lay her down and leave. She would immediately begin sobbing again as I left the room.

After doing this several times, I was getting weary. I remember standing in the hall and everything in me wanted to say, "It's okay, baby," and hold her and comfort her.

But as I stood there, the Lord used this moment to speak to me. He showed me that there would be times when I would feel like Mary. I would wonder why He was not there for me, why He was not answering my cries, and if He really loved me.

In those times, my faith would be tested. Would I trust Him and His love in the times when I didn't understand? Did I really believe that He was there without feeling Him there? Did I believe He is loving, and that he cares? Did I trust Him to take care of me? As His child, did I believe He was a good Father or would I get angry and take things into my own hands and do things my own way?

Now years later, I can tell you that even in the times when I have cried myself to sleep, times when I've screamed out, "What is going on? Where are you, God?" He has never left me. He is faithful and His Word is true. Deuteronomy 31:6 says, "He will not leave you nor forsake you," and we can count on that.

I know what it means now when we sing songs like "My feet are on the Rock." Having a foundation of sand may seem good enough until the storm comes, but it is a slippery place to be when the winds are blowing, and the storm has surrounded you. Jesus Christ is the only firm foundation.

If you have never put your trust in Jesus, I am not going to tell you it is a journey with no difficult times. We live in a tough world that is full of evil. But I will tell you that He created you with a purpose, and He loves you—big time! He loves us more than we can comprehend! He has big plans for you, but it will take surrender and trust.

I guess I could've gone into Mary's room and told her that in the end, this was all for her good, but I know she would not have understood. It would not have helped. As His child, I have to believe God is smarter than me, He loves me, and He will take care of me. That is faith and that is enough.

DIGGING DEEPER

Read James 1:2-4

1. According to this passage, when troubles come our way, what should our response be and why?

2. What do you think it means to fully surrender and trust God in difficult times when answers seem far away? Why are surrender and trust so important to faith?

3. What things do you know to be true about God that can sometimes be hard to remember when "God doesn't answer?" List any that come to mind here:

PRAYER

Father God, I believe that you are a good and perfect Father who loves me like no other. But when I am alone and crying in the dark, it can be hard to feel that truth. When I experience difficulties and pain in life, reassure me with the fact that you promised to never leave me alone in the dark. Help me to find strength in knowing that no matter what things may look like, you will work them out for my good when I fully trust you. So, help me to see the struggles in life as an opportunity to grow in my faith. I will persevere. I will endure. I will grow and I will feel hope again because I am secure in you, and you are faithful.

AMEN

Part Three

Legacy Stories
By Nancy Painter unless otherwise indicated

This section contains five true family legacy stories. You are here for a purpose and your life matters! What will your legacy be?

Memories of my Mom

Ruby, Ruby Dooby-doo, and Mom were just a few of her names. Often, she would sign her little notes to us "Mombo" with XOXO at the end. I don't ever remember calling her "mother." It was too formal for us. For some reason as she grew older, Mama seemed more appropriate—I don't know why.

I miss her.

When we were young, we lived in a big, cold, drafty farmhouse. On cold winter mornings, we would run downstairs from our bedrooms to the kitchen. There, before a warm stove, were chairs placed with our clothes carefully laid out for us, so we could dress by its warmth.

My sister, Patty, Mom and me.

I remember when I was young, she made me sit at the table until I drank all my milk. After a few times of rebellion, I learned to drink it fast because if it sat too long, it would get warm and taste even worse! I still don't like milk, except on cereal or with chocolate mixed in it. But my mom wanted to make sure I'd grow up healthy, with strong bones, so she refused to give in to my resistance.

Summer vacations were often spent at our Grandpa and Grandma Smith's cabin on Lake Chetac near Birchwood, Wisconsin. Our days were filled with fishing, swimming, floating on innertubes in the lake, drinking cold water from the pump outside of the cabin, and of course, I'll never forget the smelly outhouse.

My sister Patty, Grandpa, and me.

In the evening, our grandma often fried the most delicious fresh fish—perch, bluegill, walleye, bass, or whatever we had caught.

After dinner, we would often play rummy around the kitchen table, no television or cell phones, just talking and laughing.

My sister Lorraine, me, and my mom.

On one of our vacations, my mom and I were sitting at the end of a pier, talking, and taking in the views and fresh air. She said to me, "Nancy, love people and use things and never get the two mixed up." I don't remember much else about that conversation or the vacation, but I knew, even though I was young, that what she said was important. Her tone was serious, and I have never forgotten it.

Once in a while, Mom would save enough money so that we could splurge and go to the movies. She would allow us to choose whether to walk to the movies or take the bus. But if we walked, we could stop for a sundae at the Sweet Shop on Seventh Street on our way home. Of course, we always chose to walk!

We had fun together! I remember her rolling down hills with us at Sinnissippi Park and laughing all the way!

When I turned sixteen, she insisted that I get a part-time job. I was scared because I was terribly shy, but it helped me to grow and learn. During my teenage years, I tried sassing her back once. She walked across the room and slapped my mouth. I was surprised, and it never happened again. I'm thankful now that she never allowed me to disrespect her.

I always felt loved. I was always proud of her. I never remember hearing her swear. She was a lady, but she had spunk. She would stand up and defend me when she felt it was warranted, but she also corrected me when I needed it.

She took us to church on Sundays. She taught me to tell the truth, not to gossip, to be kind and polite, to pick good friends, and make my bed in the morning. I learned to work hard and be responsible. She taught me how to cook and clean and to always do my best, to honor God, and hundreds of other things, big and small. I could never fully express how grateful I am for all she taught me through her words and her example.

My mom worked hard and went to work every day, yet she kept our home in order. We were expected to do our part. She achieved and believed in excellence. She studied Steno-graph (machine shorthand) at home after working all day to improve on her job. She became President of the Honenegah Chapter of the National Secretaries Association and President of the Future Secretaries Association. She always looked sharp and dressed professionally and yet, she was tenderhearted and kind.

After my parents divorced, I sometimes would see her sitting at the kitchen table in the morning reading a devotional, *Our Daily Bread*. Even though this time in her life was hard, she always kept going.

Eventually, she met and married Elmer. They both worked hard but often would go dancing with friends or do something fun when the weekend arrived. After retiring, they bought a place in Florida and became "snowbirds," leaving the cold winters behind. They lived a full life.

Mom and Daddy

When Alzheimer's attacked her mind and eventually her body, she was still pleasant and sweet. Once when I took her to the grocery store with me, as she held onto the cart, she began dancing to the music playing in the store. This made me smile. She seemed so carefree. She always loved to dance!

Mom and Elmer

Elmer told us about a day they went to the grocery store, but it started raining hard. They stayed in their van waiting for it to let up. Finally, Elmer said, "Ruby, let's make a run for it!" They jumped out of the van, Elmer heading towards the store, and my mom running in another direction! He chased her down and soaking wet, they went home to change their clothes. Elmer laughed with us as he remembered that day, but he said at the time it happened, it wasn't all that funny!

It wasn't long after this that my mom came to stay at our home. It became too much for Elmer, as he developed some health issues, but he would come over regularly and pick her up for a "date." He often would bring an item of her jewelry with him. She would be surprised and "light up."

Sometimes they would go for a drive looking at places they used to live, or go to a store and out to eat. They would hold hands because they loved each other, but it also kept her from getting away from him and wandering off. She moved faster than him!

Even though it was difficult watching as my mom's mind faded, her sweet spirit was very evident to all, and there were many happy times amidst it all.

There is so much more I could say and many pictures I'd like to share, but what I want to do is to honor her. Her legacy will live on forever.

My mom grew up believing in God, and in her later years, she gave her heart to Jesus and was born again. I look forward to the day when I can hug her again in Heaven and tell her how much I love her. Maybe then I will have the words that are needed to express my love.

Memories of Daddy

We awoke in the middle of the night to the phone ringing. As I struggled to wake up and answer the call, a feeling of dread came upon me. Calls in the middle of the night are never good unless someone is having a baby. The call was to inform us that they were taking my dad by ambulance to the hospital. As we rushed to get dressed, fear gripped my heart. My dad had not been sick. It was hard for me to process all that was happening. After arriving at the hospital, we found that my dad was not responsive.

Our family gathered together. The doctors ran tests, but it did not look good. He was in a coma and they told us there wasn't any brain activity. There was a constant flow of family and friends over the next two weeks as we comforted each other, prayed, and sometimes cried together. We took shifts, day and night; there was always a family member at the hospital. There were no strict visiting hours for us, and they allowed us to go back to his room at any time.

I couldn't remember when it was that we had gotten together with my dad and family last, but I knew that we had hugged and said, "I love you," because I don't ever remember parting without those words being said to each other. I'm so very thankful for that.

One day as I was sitting in the waiting room, I became angry. I was fighting a battle inside of me. My dad was a good man and a kind man, and I thought he had a relationship with Jesus, but now I needed to know for sure. He could not die without me knowing where he would spend eternity. That day I decided to go back to his room and pray a prayer of faith for him to be healed. No devil in hell was going to steal my dad before his time without a fight. I walked down the hall to his room ready to battle for him. As I walked up to his room, the door was closed. That had never happened before. I thought that the nurses were probably taking care of him, and I decided to come back later.

As I headed back to the waiting room, I noticed a group of young teenagers who were visiting someone. The room was overflowing with people. It seemed unusual to me for so many people to be in one room. I continued to walk down the hall when I heard them all begin to sing the song *When We All Get to Heaven*. The music flowed down the hallway, and I stood there transfixed, unable to move forward. The words resonated in my heart. They sang of seeing Jesus, rejoicing, and shouting the victory when we arrive in heaven. I just stood there as people walked by me. The presence of the Lord surrounded me. I can't explain it, but there was a knowing inside of me that my dad was going to heaven. And there was an engulfing peace. I don't understand that either, but everything was settled.

The battle was over. I had my answer—my dad belonged to Jesus and was on his way to heaven. I knew he was safe, and the wrestling in my heart was over. It was only a couple of days later and my dad was gone.

It's amazing to me how when we suffer great loss if we reach out to God, He will comfort us in ways we can't imagine. As we were going to make preparations for his funeral, a song I had never heard came on the radio, *No More Night*. Its lyrics described heaven, where all things are new and there is no evil; a place where there will be no more pain or tears, or crying.

It was so beautiful! I cried in the car; my tears were a mixture of sadness and joy. I wanted my dad here, but yet I knew he was in such a wonderful place, it was hard for me to wish him to come back. I knew he was happier than he had ever experienced here on this earth.

My Dad and Dona on left.
Aunt Grace on right.

My dad was a good dad and a kind man. He was well-liked and friendly. He worked in sales at Ideal Uniform. After retiring, he and his wife, Dona, owned and operated the Maid-Rite restaurant in Loves Park, Illinois for several years. I remember how delicious the Maid-Rite sandwiches were and on St. Patrick's Day, he made the best corned beef and cabbage! They made many lifetime friends while working in this business together.

I have many wonderful memories of my dad, and I always knew deep inside me that Daddy loved me.

I remember one day when I was a little girl, falling off my bike onto the gravel driveway. My dad came running and picked me up and held me as I cried on his shoulder. It's funny how when you look back, there are moments that stand out. Yet the events all around those moments are gone. Almost like a photograph of that memory and that particular time. I felt protected by him.

He was a hero, not only to me but as a soldier in World War II. He was a brave and honorable man who received a Bronze Star for his courage. He sometimes had nightmares from his experiences in the war while serving to keep us free.

My Dad is the middle soldier.

I've heard people say about a loved one, "He was a good man. He served in the army. I'm sure he's in heaven." Or "She was such a great mom and always went to church. I'm sure she's in heaven." That sounds reasonable, but the truth is if

PFC. RAYMOND P. LAYNG

Bronze Star Awarded to Pfc. Raymond P. Layng

For his heroism in forcing two Germans manning a machine gun to surrender, an action which resulted in his company obtaining its objective, Pfc. Raymond P. Layng, 3749 Park Ridge road, has been awarded the bronze star.

Private Layng, an infantryman with the 34th Infantry division, is the son of Mr. and Mrs. Oral W. Layng, and has a brother, Irving, who is on duty with the navy in Washington, D. C.

It was in Italy on Oct. 7, 1944, that Pfc. Layng distinguished himself as related in the following citation, signed by Maj. Gen. Charles L. Bolte:

"During an attack on an enemy-held house, Pfc. Layng's platoon approached to within 75 yards of the house and then were stopped by enemy machine gun fire from positions near the house.

"While two of his comrades went to knock out one machine gun, Private Layng approached to the left by himself.

"In spite of enemy machine gun fire directed at him, Private Layng crawled out of a ditch to within 15 yards of the enemy dugout, threw four grenades and forced the two Germans manning the machine gun to surrender.

"The enemy manning the other gun withdrew and the objective was taken. The courage and aggressiveness displayed by Private Layng were exemplary and a credit

that's all it takes, why would Jesus have to die for us? Why would He have to go through all that suffering if all we have to do is live a good life to have a home in heaven? The Bible tells us we have all fallen short and there's only one way to heaven. We must be born again. (See page 268.)

I later learned that my dad had accepted Jesus in his heart when an Evangelism Explosion team came to his home and he prayed with them. He filled out a card with the date of his salvation on it. He signed it and carried it in his billfold from that day until he left this earth.

Several months after my dad died, I was downtown at the Bible Bookstore. As I walked around the store, I looked up and there was a picture of a man entering heaven and Jesus was wrapping his arms around him. I will never forget that day. To me, it was a picture of my dad being embraced by Jesus. He was welcoming him home!

Wow! What a celebration that will be when we are reunited with our family and friends! I know my dad will be there. He will be waiting for me and will wrap his arms around me and give me all the hugging I need! I'm so thankful I know that. There is not a doubt in my heart that we are going to have a joyful reunion unlike anything we have ever experienced here on Earth. We will celebrate and dance for joy! How about you? Are you ready?

Memories of Dona

Dona was my stepmom, but I prefer to think of her as my "bonus mom." She impacted all of us who knew her in different, but always positive ways. Whenever I was with her, I would come away feeling encouraged, accepted, and loved.

Her pastor told us that her Bible was underlined with many passages that were important to her. I can't remember her preaching to me or telling me how I should live my life, but she lived the life of a godly woman before us, and it spilled over onto everyone who was around her. She was a gift to all of us and her legacy and influence will not be forgotten.

My sister Laurie, Dona and brother Dale.

My brother and nephew spoke at her funeral service. They shared their memories and captured who Dona was and how she lived.

My brother Dale Layng shared a few of his many wonderful memories:

Mom lived a blessed life, 83 years of happy and healthy living. She loved God, her family, her friends, her church, her work, and her retirement. Mom told me that most of her family died young—so every day past 50 was a bonus. While she was in her 70's, Mom would tell me, "I am going to see the oldies." She just didn't feel old. She told me, "I feel like I am in my twenties until I look in the mirror."

Mom loved our family home. She lived there for 47 years. It was a two-story home on top of a hill with forty-three windows. It was warm in the winter and cool in the summer. I always felt safe there. A typical Saturday would consist of a cool breeze coming through the windows, a Cub's game on in the corner of the room, and friends and neighbors popping in and out.

- Mom always had change for a candy bar.
- Yearly fishing vacations consisted of cabin living and fish fries every night.
- I always had an awesome bike.
- Sunday meals often included a friend or relative.
- Everyone was welcome there. Come as you are.
- Mom was always teaching, and always encouraging.
- I enjoyed risk—jumping off the roof, riding a mini-bike, jumping my bike over ramps, and barefoot water skiing. Mom would often say, "Okay, I just don't want to watch."

- Mom attended my baseball games for 48 years. I love that Mom attended my hockey games, Mom in her eighties and me in my fifties.
- When Dad came home, he would go right to Mom for a kiss. Mom and Dad really loved each other. When Dad passed away, she said, "Well, that's it. He is my husband." She never remarried.

After my Aunt Jan retired, Mom spent a lot of time running errands and on adventures with her. Mom and I would share plans each morning. Often, I would say (respectfully), "You kids have fun. Love you."

I found a little Bible in Mom's car. It is a bit worn, but only one verse is underlined. (It is marked with a Culver's free scoop card.) Revelation 1:17-18. "And when I saw Him, I fell at His feet as dead. But he laid his right hand on me, saying to me, 'Do not be afraid; I am the First and the Last. I am He who lives, and was dead, and behold I am alive forevermore. Amen. And I have the keys of Hades and of Death." **Mom is with Christ!"**

My dad, Dona,
Dale and sister Laurie

254

My nephew Jason Layng shared the three words that came to mind when he thought of his grandma.

GODLY — My grandmother was the epitome of Godly. She hid scripture in her heart and truly lived her life according to God's plan. I once had a homework assignment asking two questions. The first question was, "Does God have the ability to change his mind.?" The second was, "What does heaven look like?" So, I called my grandma and without hesitation, she rattled off about twenty Scriptures to look up. Although I wasn't a straight-A student, she helped me ace that assignment.

She never had to speak to show people who God was--you could see Him by the way she lived.

GIVING — My grandma would give you all the money in her purse and still ask what else she could do for you, as long as it could get a smile, or take the stress off your shoulders. For many years, she would take my sister and me out on Friday nights just to give my parents a breather from our shenanigans. She would take us on

Dona teaching Sunday school

255

adventures and pay money to sit and watch us do something. It made her truly happy. We never ended the night without a treat.

GRACIOUS — to which Google's definition is "showing divine grace." My grandmother had this grace because of her foundation in Christ—no doubt. No matter where you were or are in life, she would find the good and positive and remind you of it. She came to all my sporting events from soccer to Rockford's First softball games—eleven years of softball games.

During one of my tournaments, a thrown ball went rogue, hitting my grandma in her arm and side leaving a wild bruise. That wasn't going to stop her. She was there the following week in full catcher's gear in her chair ready to root for us.

If life was a game of baseball, she may not have known she was in the ninth inning, but she hit the ball out of the park with the way she lived!

And so now that you've rounded third and made it home, thank you, Gram, for the impact you've left on all of us. So, until we meet again...I love you.

The Love Story of David & Patty

Hollywood has its versions of "love stories." Usually, they are pretty shallow, based mostly on emotion, physical attraction, and superficial storylines. It's sad to say, but they are poor examples to our children. There are love stories that need to be told that are filled with commitment, unselfishness, values, family, and fun. These are the real love stories. This is one of those stories, the story of my sister, Patty, and her husband, David.

The first time I met Dave was the night he took my little sister, Patty, to their senior prom. He came to the door of our home dressed for the prom. He was a tall, brown-haired, blue-eyed Italian/Irish boy. Patty was a petite auburn-haired blue-eyed Swedish/English/Irish girl. They made a really cute couple.

As I remember, this was her first date and the only guy she ever dated. She told me when he looked at her with his big blue eyes and contagious smile, it was all over! There was no competition. He was the one! She never dated anyone else.

They graduated from high school, and it was only a couple of years later that they were married. Their first home was a mobile home, but Dave was a hard worker and a great provider. They lived there for a couple of years and then bought a two-family home and rented out the lower apartment to help make the payment. They worked hard and later were able to purchase a single-family home.

Patty had gone to college for a couple of years because she wanted to become a teacher. That was her gifting. She loved to teach. Dave became an electrician apprentice.

It wasn't long before their first child, Michelle, was born. She was followed closely by Trina. A few years later another

Trina, David, Patty and Michelle

daughter, Sari was born. Finally, a son, Paul was born and their family was complete.

Patty put her dream of teaching on hold to be a full-time mom and homemaker. That was her priority. Dave became a union electrician. My husband, being a pipefitter, worked on jobs with David several times. He always enjoyed working with him, as he told me Dave was a man of integrity. He was well-liked and very smart.

Patty was raised in the Lutheran faith and David was raised Catholic, but they loved each other very much. It was something they would work through. They started visiting various churches to find one that they both could feel was right for them. While visiting one of these churches they were born again, and they decided that would be where their family would attend, worship, and grow.

They were a tight-knit family. They stuck together and had fun together. For a time, my family, our grandmother, and their family all lived on the same street. My two children would go to their home after school until I got off work. I remember walking in and there was always the wonderful smell of food cooking and a relaxed and loving atmosphere.

Sari, Patty, Trina, Michelle, David and Paul

When Dave was in his 30's, he was diagnosed with rheumatoid arthritis. It had a devastating effect on his body, and he was in a lot of pain. Sometimes it was hard for him to even get out of bed in the morning. But this disease could not stop him. He continued to work. The disease did not become a part of his identity. He would not allow it to dominate his life. I don't ever remember him complaining.

Patty went back to school, finished her education, and taught at a Christian school for several years until they both retired. They raised a beautiful family and have several grandchildren.

Dave passed away after a short, unexpected illness. It was a tremendous loss to all. I visited with my sister, and she shared a beautiful story of God comforting her. She's allowed me to share this in hopes that it may encourage someone who is also going through loss.

This is an excerpt from her journal.

Last night, feeling very lonesome, but know that this is not my permanent home—Heaven is; but this is the only home I've known. Paid for a headstone and thought this home I know won't be the same ever again because Dave isn't here and that's final. Realizing God knows my thoughts and emotions I asked Him to please help me with this end—so final—loss of Dave. This thought came into my mind immediately and made me smile: He just beat you home again!

Dave and I would come from jobs (he from Dekalb and me from Christian Life School) and would meet for dinner at Cherry Valley Cafe sometimes before coming home. I'd say, "Meet you at home," and his answer was to smile with his eyes twinkling and say, "Beat you home." I'd tell him I wasn't racing and he'd grin and say, "That's what losers say," or "Chicken." He'd usually beat me home, but once in a while I'd get home first and let him know I'd won, to which he'd smile and say, "Thought you weren't racing."

I wasn't, but if I saw I was ahead, I'd hurry into the garage. Wonderful fun we had with everyday life. God, I miss him so much and I thank you for the smile from remembering this and how he liked to beat me home—He beat you home again.

Dave and Patty were married for 46 years. I know she is thankful that he is no longer in pain, but it is hard, and she misses him every day. It helps her to remember that picture the Lord gave her of him standing at the door of his eternal home with a smile on his face and a twinkle in his eye, waiting for her. Their story is not over. They will have all eternity to catch up and be together.

We are so thankful that God understands and helps us through our times of great loss. Psalm 34:18 ESV says "The Lord is near to the brokenhearted and saves the crushed in spirit." Psalms 147:3 ESV says, "He heals the brokenhearted and binds up their wounds." These are our promises!

While at the airport one day, Patty and Dave heard a song on the elevator that they liked and spontaneously decided to dance to it. Their granddaughter, Ana, snapped their picture.

This is a true love story, a story of Dave and Patty's love for each other, for their family, and for God. This is their legacy.

A Tribute to Dale W. Layng

by Jason Layng

When you write about someone, you usually pick out highlights from their life, or spectacular moments that flood your memories. But this is going to be a little different. This small excerpt is going to be about my dad's character.

My father did everything in his power to give my sister and me the life he could dream of. There were many things in life that he wanted, like motorcycles, boats, or even more extravagant vacations. But instead of that, he bought me soccer cleats, hockey gear, and my sister a Mustang.

My dad was always the coolest guy in the room even if he didn't say anything. Everyone that ever saw him play a sport or fix something around the house knew of his extreme capabilities to be the best.

He used every moment in life as a teaching lesson for me and my sister, Angela. He taught us when to speak up and when to hold back. He taught me when to forgive and just move away from trouble, as well as when to attack it and overcome it. But mostly, he taught me how to endure, and no matter the level of stress, to continue worshiping Jesus.

Dad, Me (Jason), and Angie

He was a Godly man that seemed to have life figured out, even when he didn't. I have yet to meet someone that would give up as much as he did just to see his kids smile. He was our teacher, our financial stability, our emotional support, and best of all he was "DAD."

My dad's encouraging voice still rings in my ears to this day. I can hear him yelling 'C'MON BUD" when I rounded second base because I happened to burn the outfielder. I can hear him telling my sister to "open it up" in her brand-new Mustang.

He has truly taught me how a Christian man should live, not only through words but through his actions.

Dad, I am still deeply pained to this day that you are gone, but because I am fully confident of your relationship with God, I know we will meet up again.

I love you pops and can't wait to see you again!
Your son, Jason

Me (Jason), Dad, and my sister Angie

What's Your Legacy?

DIGGING DEEPER

1. What positive memory, lesson, or example do you have from your childhood upbringing that has helped to shape you as a person?

2. Name a specific challenge you faced growing up that helped you to learn and become stronger.

3. Who is someone who has had a big influence in your life?

266

4. What is something they have taught you that you would like to pass on?

5. Is there a specific thing you can do or say this week (or even today!) to a loved one to intentionally express your love and appreciation for them?

PRAYER

Dear God, thank you for the loved ones you have placed in my life! Show me how to love and honor each of them so that they really know how much they are loved and valued. Teach me how to live in such a way that the legacy I leave behind will be a gift and a blessing to those who knew me. Heavenly Father, as your child, help me to know and experience you in true and deep ways so that my life will be an expression of your love.

AMEN

Part Four

Jesus is Asking

Are you discouraged with religion and looking for a relationship? This section has the answers you may be searching for!

Jesus Is Asking,
"Will You Be Mine?"

HOW DO I BECOME HIS?

GOD LOVES YOU

"For God so loved the world, that he gave his only Son, that <u>whoever</u> believes in Him should not perish but have eternal life." John 3:16

"But God shows His love for us in that while we were still sinners, Christ died for us." Romans 5:8

ALL ARE SINNERS

"For all have sinned and fall short of the glory of God." Romans 3:23

"As it is written: "None is righteous, no, not one." Romans 3:10

GOD'S REMEDY FOR SIN

"For the wages of sin is death, but the free gift of God is eternal life in Christ Jesus our Lord." Romans 6:23

"But to all who did receive him, who believed in His Name, He gave the right to become children of God." John 1:12

ALL MAY BE SAVED NOW

"Behold I stand at the door and knock. If anyone hears my voice and opens the door, I will come in to him." Revelation 3:20

"For everyone who calls on the name of the Lord will be saved." Romans 10:13

ABOVE SCRIPTURES FROM THE ENGLISH STANDARD VERSION (ESV)

WRITE IN YOUR OWN WORDS WHAT EACH OF THE SCRIPTURES YOU READ SAYS TO YOU

GOD LOVES YOU_____

_____

_____

ALL ARE SINNERS_____

_____

_____

GOD'S REMEDY FOR SIN_____

_____

_____

ALL MAY BE SAVED NOW_____

_____

_____

My Decision to Receive Christ as My Savior

MY PRAYER (This is an example of a prayer inviting Jesus into your life.)

Today, Father God, I ask you to forgive me of my sins. Thank you for sending Jesus Christ to die for me on the cross. I thank You that He is alive now, and I ask You, Jesus, to come into my heart and live in me. Take control of my life—be my Lord, my Savior and my Friend.

_____

Name

_____

Date

If you prayed this prayer, what's next?

Now that you have accepted Jesus into your heart and life, here are some tips that will help you grow in your faith and continue this amazing journey that God has for you.

1. Read your Bible a little (or a lot) every day. It is God's love letter to you. He wants you to get to know Him on a very personal level. A good place to start is the

book of John in the New Testament. Some people make the mistake of starting in the book of Genesis to read through the Bible. The Old Testament is written before Jesus came to earth to rescue us. It is the inspired Word of God and is filled with wonderful true stories of men and women of God. It has wisdom and truth, but it can also be a confusing place to start. There is much treasure waiting for you to find as you read His Word.

2. Finding a Bible-believing church is very important. Making friends who will encourage you on this new journey is very important to growing and succeeding. Following Jesus is exciting, but not always easy in the world we live in daily. The church is also a place for you to help and encourage others. God has created you with giftings and talents that will be a blessing to others.

3. Don't forget to invite Him along as you make everyday decisions. He is waiting to talk with you and loves you like no other!

Acknowledgments

There are no words to express our thankfulness to God for His goodness and love, for His restoration power, and for His forgiveness and mercy.

God orchestrated our story, but many of you had big and small parts to play in it. No one makes it through times of heartache and trouble alone. We are so thankful for all those who have held out their hands and shared their heart with us on this journey.

Thank you to...

My daughter Denise for her belief in me, her unconditional love, and for always being there. I don't believe this book would have happened without her encouragement and help. Poco a poco! My daughter Mary for cheering me on when I needed to keep going, for her love, and for believing in me! *Mom*

David and Lindy Meyer for walking through it all with me. *Ray*

Amy Muranko Gahan for encouraging me to move forward when I hadn't begun to start. My friend Ann Crews, for her faith, insight, and belief in me. My friend Margie Hartman for her help in a really rough time. *Nancy*

Warren and Judy Freedlund, for their unconditional love and support and for welcoming, with open arms, my new wife into the family.

Bill and Mary Ching for the original inspiration and title for our book.

And thank you to all our children and their spouses in our blended family who continue to love and bless us. You are an encouragement and have been an inspiration to us—David, Jonathan, Denise and Tim, Joe and Melanie, Aaron and Melinda, Les and Mindy, David and Lindy, Mary and Joseph, Richie and Ariel. We love you all!

Our grandchildren who have accepted their new Grandpa and Grandma with outstretched arms: Jonathan, Allison, Adler, Mika, Max, Brayden, Zachary, Alexandria, Raedyn, Janelle, Jadon and Parker.

Our great-grandchildren who are an extra blessing in our lives: Amara, Michael, and Rayna.

A special thank you to Mika Monson for contributing her artwork and to Max Monson for his help in the editing of this book.

Also, thank you to Jennifer Crosswhite of Tandem Services as she also provided some editing services for our book.

Apostle Don Lyon and Pastor Donna Lyon, Kellie Symonds, Brad and Carla Hampton, Margaret Byers, and all of the Faith Center family.

Pastor Josh Amstutz for his encouragement and our church family at Lakeland Community Church!

With sincere love and gratitude,
Ray and Nancy

About the Authors

Ray and Nancy Painter live in Wisconsin, across the street from beautiful Lake Delavan. After they married, they enrolled in Rhema Bible College and graduated two years later. They have been involved in jail ministry, and home Bible study groups, and are part of the Gideon International Ministry.

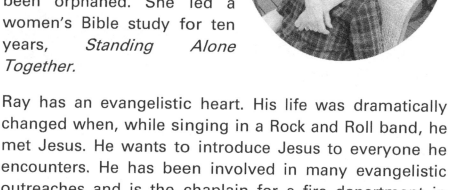

Nancy has a heart for women who have been wounded by life and children who have been orphaned. She led a women's Bible study for ten years, *Standing Alone Together.*

Ray has an evangelistic heart. His life was dramatically changed when, while singing in a Rock and Roll band, he met Jesus. He wants to introduce Jesus to everyone he encounters. He has been involved in many evangelistic outreaches and is the chaplain for a fire department in Wisconsin. He and Nancy are also involved in a nursing home ministry.

They have a blended family which includes nine children, twelve grandchildren, three great-grandchildren, and their Shih Poo dog, Tuxie. Ray retired from being a pipefitter and a business owner, and Nancy retired from her job as the church receptionist. They are now free to enjoy their ever-growing family and pursue other life interests.

They have never written a book before and share their story with the hope that it encourages others whose lives may not have turned out the way they expected them to. You can reach them at whataboutnancy@gmail.com or visit www.whataboutnancy.com.

Denise Monson is an office manager for Global Impact Ministries & Outreach Association (www.myglobal.org) and also operates a bookkeeping business.

Her goal is to share the hope of Jesus through these devotionals and in everyday life. She is a wife and mother of two.

She was born in California and raised in Northern Illinois. Since her children are now "grown-ish", she's been re-discovering hobbies like reading, biking, and kayaking with her husband. You can reach her at denise@bookkeepingit.com

About the Illustrator

Mika Monson is a film/animation/illustration major at NIU in Dekalb, IL with a focus in 3D Animation. After graduating, she plans to work in downtown Chicago in a career that utilizes her passion for art and creating. Her hometown is Winnebago, IL. You can reach her at <u>mikaraeart@gmail.com</u> or on Instagram: @mikaraeart or LinkedIn